WHAT TO READ, AND HOW TO READ,

BEING

CLASSIFIED LISTS OF CHOICE READING,

WITH

APPROPRIATE HINTS AND REMARKS,

ADAPTED TO THE GENERAL READER, TO SUBSCRIBERS TO LIBRARIES, AND TO PERSONS INTENDING TO FORM COLLECTIONS OF BOOKS.

BROUGHT DOWN TO SEPTEMBER, 1870.

BY

CHARLES H. MOORE, M. D.,

FORMERLY PROFESSOR IN OAKLAND COLLEGE, MISSISSIPPI, AND IN BALTIMORE CITY COLLEGE.

NEW YORK:
D. APPLETON AND COMPANY,
90, 92 & 94 GRAND STREET.
1871.

CONTENTS.

	PAGE
INTRODUCTION	9
HINTS	11
EXPLANATORY	14
I.—History—Ancient, Mediæval, and Modern . .	15
II.—Biography	32
III.—Travels Voyages	44
IV.—Natural History—Physiology, Hygiene, Botany .	59
V.—Natural Philosophy—Astronomy, Chemistry, Geology, Mineralogy	63
VI.—Philosophy (Mental and Moral)—Logic, and Theology	69
VII.—Political Economy—Social Science, Law, Political Science	72
VIII.—Devotional Works	75
IX.—Poetry	79
X.—Belles-Lettres—Philology, Criticism, Fine Arts .	86
XI.—Essays—Miscellanies, Table-Talk, Ana, Lectures, etc.	91
XII.—Memoirs, Letters—Recollections, Journals, Autobiographies, etc.	94
XIII.—Novels, Romances, and Tales	100
XIV.—Miscellaneous	121
XV.—Periodicals	129

APPENDIX.

PAGE

I.—Books of Reference 130
II.—Books for Parents and Housekeepers . . . 132
III.—Books for the Young 133
IV.—A Few Hints to those intending to enter Business, or any of the Professions or Trades . . . 137
V.—Additional Works for a Library 140
VI.—Modern Languages 146
VII.—Assumed or Changed Names 148
VIII.—A Few Anonymous Works, with Names of Authors, real or imputed 151

INTRODUCTION.

The title-page of this book indicates, with perhaps sufficient exactness, the chief points in its *aim and plan.* A glance through the Table of Contents, and the Synopsis, will give a still clearer and fuller idea. It will be seen that, in order to add to the efficiency of the classified lists as exhibited in the synopsis, an effort has been made to adapt them to readers of different ages; also, to those whose leisure is more or less abundant. The importance of this feature need not be dwelt upon.

The *utility* of some guide to the inexperienced reader to direct and shape his studies amid the immense mass of literature now before the public, is something so evident that it is unnecessary to enter into any labored argument in its proof. To parents also, who may not have time or ability to select properly the reading of their children, the benefits and convenience of a work like the present are undeniable. But, as regards utility, there is another view still more significant. The deplorable effects of modern sensational literature upon the *intellect* as well as the morals of the present generation, is a matter of common observation. To counteract the influence of vile or worthless books, something better must be offered, something which will please as well as instruct, which will refine the taste and evoke the nobler emotions. In the present volume something has been done, it is hoped, toward attaining this end.

However unpretending this manual may be, the author is not the less sensible of its liability to unfavorable criticism. It may, especially, be objected that the question, How to read? has been treated too cursorily. In explanation, it is proper to state that the work has been written subject to various antagonistic conditions. For instance, the author aimed to make it sufficiently large to be of substantial service as a catalogue for subscribers to libraries, etc.; at the same time small enough to admit of being published at a moderate price. Again, while seeking to embrace the really standard literature in the English tongue—as far as adapted to the general reader—regard had to be paid to the accessibility of the books cited. At all events, whatever may be its defects, the author can say with truth that he has spared neither time nor conscientious care. Should it succeed in affording assistance to the aspiring student, or in tempting others to exchange the vicious or the unprofitable for something of enduring worth, he trusts that the good thus effected will win indulgence for venial errors.

HINTS.

1. Rigid "plans" and "courses of reading" are seldom of use. In fact, they are, in general, positively injurious; for, as they are rarely carried out, they disgust the reader with system in any shape, and dishearten him for further efforts. If formed at all, programmes cannot be too simple and elastic. They will then stand some chance of being followed. We have the authority of two great names for this piece of advice—Dr. Johnson and Sir Walter Scott.

2. Upon commencing any book, it will be found highly useful to have a sheet of blank paper upon which to mark the number of the page, and, if needed, the paragraph, where any thing is met demanding further investigation, or reperusal. If the reader keeps a commonplace-book he will find this by far the most convenient mode for entering any thing desired.

3. Have always a book or two, to take up at intervals of leisure. The odd minutes thus employed will count profitably at the end of a year, and will pleasantly occupy time which might otherwise be spent impatiently, or with *ennui.* Some French author, whose name has escaped me, was enabled in this way to compose a work of high reputation.

4. Devise some plan by means of which you may stow up in compact and systematic form the fruits of your reading, observation, etc. This is a great help to the memory, and a valuable aid to our researches upon any particular subject.

5. A few books—but the *best* and *slowly read*—will be found more profitable than ten times the number badly selected, especially if read hastily.

6. Choose some one book to be read over and over. Let the

author selected depend on your own taste, but be sure he is no second-rate one. The Bible, Shakespeare, Bacon, Milton, Blackstone, Montaigne, Plato, might be mentioned as suitable for this purpose of constant and special study. A thorough and familiar acquaintance with even one sterling book is a source of infinite pleasure and benefit. Besides, the process of gaining this familiar acquaintance is in itself an excellent mental training.

7. Make it a rule to *reflect*, *write*, and *converse*, upon what you read; also, to *review* your reading frequently and regularly. It will be found of great utility to make brief abstracts of books read, with thoughts, remarks, etc. The length of these abstracts would, naturally, be regulated by the intrinsic worth of the book. Observe, this writing of abstracts compels more or less reflection and reviewing.

8. Avoid all books which are *trashy*, "*smart*," or, if I may apply the epithet to a book, *cunning*. Ruskin tells us: "A common book will often give much amusement; it is only a noble book which will give dear friends."

9. In studying any subject, or in examining into any question, bear in mind it is the *truth—the real facts*—which is the object of inquiry; so, lay aside beforehand all preconceived ideas not well based—opinions grounded on personal sympathy or early education—on popular clamor or national prejudice, etc. Hear both sides.

10. Avoid *narrow*, *exclusive* reading. This dwarfs alike the intellect and the judgment, not to mention the amount of literary enjoyment thus lost. Let books of imagination as well as of facts—of speculative thought as well as of positive science—have a portion of your attention.

11. To carry out the last hint, let me recommend a judicious distribution of time between *prose* and *poetry*.

12. Don't neglect *old* authors. The taste which craves only the latest book out is absurd as well as vicious.

13. Don't skip the *preface* of a book. The preface often furnishes valuable insight into the character both of the author and his performance.

14. To those about commencing scientific studies, for instance, chemistry, astronomy, etc., I would suggest *not to begin* with a

long and formal text-book. Choose rather something short and pleasant; if possible, something treating of a *single* branch. A variety of works of this description, carefully selected with this purpose in view, will be found under the different heads.

15. *Exclusive newspaper or magazine reading* is ruinous, be assured, to healthy intellectual training, and to the acquisition of knowledge.

16. Although the *better class of books* may seem, at first, heavy and hard to understand, with a little resolution and perseverance the difficulties will disappear; and, once the author's meaning is readily grasped, the reader's previous distaste will also disappear; a sense of the immense superiority of the truly great writer will be opened to his perception, and, besides all this, the pleasure derived will be proportionably increased. I make this remark with particular reference to poetry and works of fiction.

17. *A Caution.*—When a book of acknowledged excellence fails to please at the first trial, the fact is generally to be attributed to the *immature* mental growth or mental cultivation of the student. The same book at a *later* period may afford the greatest delight. In a word, reading matter must be selected which is suited to the age, capacity, and state of intellectual development.

18. *Join some library society*, if there is any within reach. It would be hard to name any other source of pleasurable occupation so cheap, so profitable, and so pure. The outlay is only a few dollars, which will save, perhaps, ten times the amount. Bear in mind that a book of real worth not only pleases during its perusal, but *leaves the reader wiser and better.*

I would earnestly press upon the attention of young people living in a place where there is no public library *the importance of making a collection of books*, however small. Only make a commencement; give the experiment a trial. A collection once formed, its utility, and the gratification it yields, will soon be recognized. This matter deserves the attention of old as well as young, for it must be remembered that a well-informed community is also orderly, enterprising, and reasonable. Unless the art of reading taught in our public schools is turned to practical use, the whole system is little better than a sham.

EXPLANATORY.

I. An asterisk (*) denotes books that are *rare*, *out of print*, or *not republished* in this country; the last, however, can be ordered, though at an enhanced price.

II. A obelisk (†) denotes books suitable, as a *short course*, for readers with limited time.

III. The *initial letter* is sometimes used for the entire word, as: H. for History; L. for Life.

IV. The "Supplemental List" is composed of additional works in case the reader should wish to make further research.

SUGGESTIONS.

1. Read the Contents and Synopsis carefully, so as to get a clear idea of the arrangement of the Manual.
2. If your time is limited, select accordingly.
3. Read the introductory remarks under each head.
4. A good English Dictionary; Dictionaries of French, German, and Latin; an Encyclopædia, and a good Atlas (with index), are recommended as the first acquisitions toward a collection of books.

REMARKS.

1. I have not always followed a logical arrangement, when a different one promised some practical advantage.
2. Works consisting of *more than one* volume have generally the number stated.
3. With few exceptions, books named in the Catalogue have been published or republished in this country.
4. Books are cited by the head and section.

1.—HISTORY.

To read History with advantage, it will be found very useful to select some one good author—neither very prolix nor yet too brief—and make him the basis of more extended study. The author thus selected should be thoroughly mastered. In connection, reference more or less copious should be made to other authors who have treated the same subject from different points of view, or who have arrived at opposite conclusions. History should always be read with a good map at hand, upon which the theatres of the different events, lines of march, changes of boundary, etc., can be kept before the eye. Nothing impresses historical events more firmly upon the mind than this plan of study, which at the same time teaches geography, both physical and political. Biographies, memoirs, and travels, which throw light upon the period under consideration, the customs and social conditions of the time, or the characters of the principal actors, should be consulted. This mode of studying history gives a fulness and vividness of conception, and imparts an interest which will amply repay the student's diligence. For the profit to be derived from historical reading, see a Lecture delivered by Prof. Goldwin Smith, at the Cornell University, published in the *Atlantic Monthly* for January, 1870.

ANCIENT HISTORY.

THE JEWS.

† Smith's (Dr. W.) History of the Old Testament.

† Smith's (Dr. W.) History of the New Testament.

Milman's (Dean). History of the Jews. 3 vols. This celebrated work narrates the history of the Jewish people from the earliest antiquity down to modern times. It is characterized by unsurpassed accuracy and impartiality.

Josephus (Fl.), The Works of. His Antiquities embrace from Adam to the twelfth year of Our Lord. The Wars of the Jews refer chiefly to the contest against the Romans, and to the destruction of Jerusalem. There is also an able tract in defence of his countrymen.

Edersheim (Rev. A.). History of the Jewish Nation. Full and graphic.

Illustrative Authorities.

See Dean Stanley's works, under Section "Miscellaneous History."

EGYPT, ASSYRIA, PERSIA, Etc.

Farr (E.). History of Egypt, Assyria, Babylonia, etc. 4 vols., small 8vo.

* Rawlinson (Prof. G.). The Five Great Monarchies of the Ancient Eastern World. Embracing Chaldea, Assyria, Babylon, Media, and Persia. An admirable and interesting account of their history, geography, and antiquities.

† Le Normand and Chevalier's Student's Manual of Oriental History. From the French. To be completed in 2 vols. It is highly spoken of.

Heeren's (A. H. L.) History of the Carthaginians, Egyptians, and Ethiopians.

Kenrick's Egypt under the Pharaohs. 2 vols. [2 vols.

Sharpe's Egypt under the Ptolemies.

Sharpe's Egypt under the Romans. The last three recommended by Chancellor Kent.

Bunsen's Egypt's Place in Universal History. By a scholar of the first rank.

GREECE.

† Smith's (Dr. W.) Student's History of Greece.

Heeren's (A. H. L.) History of Greece (from the German).

Grote's (Geo.) History of Greece. 12 vols., 12mo. From the earliest times to death of Alexander the Great. This is *the* great History of Greece; unequalled not only for its accuracy, fulness, and erudition, but also for the philosophic and genial spirit with which it is imbued.

Supplemental List.

Keightley's. A good compend.

Mitford's. Interesting in style, but partisan.

† Thirlwall's. Excellent.

Ancient Historians. — Herodotus, Thucydides, Xenophon. These are the principal original sources. Translations are in Bohn's Classical Library. Prof. Rawlinson has written an admirable translation of Herodotus, enriched with valuable notes and dissertations.

Illustrative Authorities.

† Plutarch's Lives.

Williams's Life of Alexander the Great.

Travels of Anacharsis. Nearly obsolete, but entertaining and instructive.

Wordsworth's Classical Tour.

Heeren's Reflections on the Politics of Ancient Greece.

Boeckh's Public Economy of Athens. Very valuable.

Becker's Charicles. A novel, illustrating Grecian manners and customs.

ROME.

† Liddell's (H. G.) Student's History of Rome. From the earliest times to the establishment of the Empire. An excellent elementary work.

† Smith's (Dr. W.) "The Student's Gibbon." An abridgment.

† Arnold's (Dr. T.) History of Rome. 2 vols., 8vo. Highly esteemed.

Arnold's (Dr. T.) Later Roman Commonwealth. 1 vol., 8vo. Was left unfinished, owing to the author's death.

Dyer's (T. H.) History of the Kings of Rome. Written to defend the legendary or romantic history of early Rome from the attacks of Niebuhr and his school.

Mommsen's (Theodor) History of Rome. 4 vols., 8vo. Bringing the narrative down to the battle of Thapsus. This is considered the *best* History of Rome extant. The work is not yet completed. Messrs. Scribner & Co. are publishing an American edition.

Merivale's (C.) Roman History under the Empire. 7 vols., small 8vo. A truly magnificent work, marked by elegant and profound scholarship.

Gibbon's (Edward) Decline and Fall of the Roman Empire. 6 vols., 12mo. Reaching down to A. D. 1590. Best edition by W. Smith, D. D., with notes by Milman, Guizot, etc. Murray, London, 1854.

Supplemental List.

Niebuhr's, 5 vols. To the death of Constantine. Celebrated, but hardly adapted to popular taste. Niebuhr was a Dane.

Michelet's. From the French. Compendious and well arranged.

Original Authorities.—Livy, Tacitus, Sallust, Cæsar, Polybius.

Illustrative Authorities.

Plutarch's Lives.

Liddell's Life of Julius Cæsar.

* Mahon's Life of Belisarius.

Montesqnieu's. On the Greatness and Decline of the Romans. A work distinguished by its philosophic views and eloquence of style.

* Sir W. Gell's Topography of Rome.

* Eustace's Classical Tour.

Addison's Travels.

Becker's Gallus. A novel illustrating Roman domestic life.

Lockhart's Valerius.

Kingsley's Hypatia. The last two are novels of singular excellence. Hypatia was a lady of great beauty and talent, of Alexandria; fourth century.

Niebuhr's Lectures on the History of Rome.

De Quincey's Cæsars.

GENERAL HISTORY—Ancient.

Taylor's (W. C.) Manual of Ancient History. 8vo. An excellent summary.

Heeren's (A. H.) Ancient History. Peculiarly original and philosophic.

Bryce's. Holy Roman Empire. A small but most learned and valuable work, giving a thread which runs through all European history, from Cæsar to Napoleon I.

Supplemental List.

Dew's Digest of Ancient and Modern History.

Von Müller's Course of Universal History. 4 vols. Held in high estimation.

Tytler's Universal History. 6 vols.

Philip Smith's Ancient History. 3 vols., 8vo. Maps, plans, etc.

Illustrative Works on General History (Ancient). — Niebuhr's Lectures on Ancient History.

Works of Reference (Ancient History).—Long's Ancient Atlas.

Heeren's Politics, Intercourse and Trade of the Chief Nations of Antiquity. 6 volumes.

Dr. W. Smith's Smaller Classical Dictionary of the Biography, Mythology, and Geography, of the Ancients.

D. W. Smith's Smaller Dictionary of Greek and Roman Antiquities. These last two are small octavos, with maps and woodcuts.

Brown's Greek and Roman Literatures.

MEDIÆVAL HISTORY.

† Greene's History of the Middle Ages. 1 vol., 12mo.

Kœppen's (Prof. A.) World in the Middle Ages. 2 vols. A valuable and well-arranged work. There is an Historical Atlas prepared to accompany it.

Schmitz's (L.) Middle Ages. 2 vols. A judicious compend.

Hallam's (H.) State of Europe during the Middle Ages. 4 vols. With supplemental volume, published in 1848. A work justly celebrated for its research, eloquence, and impartiality.

Works of Reference.—† Gage's Modern Historical Atlas. Small 8vo. Very useful for showing the shifting boundaries of nations; also their frequent change of names.

Kœppen's Atlas of the Middle Ages.

MODERN HISTORY.

ENGLAND.

† Hume's (D.) "The Student's Hume."

* "Knight's" (C.) Popular History of England. 8 vols. A truly admirable work; embraces literature, art, social matters, etc. It is profusely illustrated.

Hume's (D.) History of England. 4 vols., 8vo. Notwithstanding a host of rivals, and in spite of undisputed partiality toward the House of Stuart, this is still regarded as the standard History of England. The original work extended only to the abdication of James II., 1688. Smollett, the novelist, supplied from his history, a continuation to George II.; and various others, Hughes, Miller, etc., have carried the narration down to late times.

Lingard's (Dr. J.) History of England. 10 vols., small 8vo. To 1688. An able and conscientious work; upholds Catholic views.

Macaulay's (Lord) History of England. 3 vols. From James II. to death of William III. Left unfinished by the early death of the author. The brilliancy of style, and the attractive manner in which the subject is treated, have given these volumes an unparalleled popularity.

Cassell's Pictorial History of England. By William Howitt. 8 vols., 8vo.

Supplemental List.

* Rapin. 12 vols. To 1688. Dull style, but accurate and impartial.

Outlines by Society for Diffusion of Useful Knowledge.

Mackintosh's. 3 vols. To death of George II. Philosophic and impartial.

Keightley's.

Lord Mahon's. 2 vols., 8vo. To the Peace of Utrecht. Edited by H. Reed. Highly esteemed.

Froude's. 12 vols. From the fall of Wolsey to the defeat of the Armada. Froude makes an ingenious and powerful defence for Henry VIII. Two American editions.

Illustrative Authorities.

Palgrave's History of the Anglo-Saxons. Convenient size, and agreeable style.

Turner's History of the Anglo-Saxons. 3 vols., 8vo. Able, but too voluminous for popular use.

Thierry's History of the Conquest of England by the Normans. From the French. Extends from 55 B. C. to early portion of Richard I.'s reign. An interesting story.

Caroline Halstead's History of Richard III. An attempt to disprove the common charges against King Richard.

Walpole's Historic Doubts on the Life and Reign of Richard III.

Carlyle's Letters and Speeches of Oliver Cromwell. Has a high reputation.

Forster's Lives of the Statesmen of the Commonwealth. 1 vol., 8vo. Of the highest character.

Forster's Life of Cromwell. Forster is esteemed as an honest, liberal, and acute writer.

Forster's Arrest of the Five Members by Charles I. Written to correct mistaken impressions about the event.

Guizot's History of the English Revolution of 1640. Dignified and trustworthy.

† Goldwin Smith's Three English Statesmen: Pym, Cromwell, and Pitt.

Towle's History of Henry the Fifth; King of England, Lord of Ireland, and Heir of France. 1 vol. 8vo.

Guizot's Monk: or, the Fall of the Republic, and Restoration of Monarchy in England, 1660.

* Mackintosh's History of the Revolution of 1688. Marked by broad and philosophic views.

Thackeray's Four Georges. Witty and satirical, but just.

Napier's History of the Peninsular War. 5 vols., 8vo. A work of sterling value.

Jesse's Memoirs of the Pretenders and their Adherents. Very pleasant reading, and fair in its judgments.

Kinglake's History of the Crimean War. 4 vols. Not yet completed.

Dr. Doran's Queens of the House of Hanover. Very dramatic, but occasionally deficient in research.

Miss Strickland's Lives of the Queens of England. 7 vols. For those who have time and inclination, an entertaining and instructive work. There is an abridgment in one volume.

* Dr. Paul's Picture of Old England. A collection of capital essays; among these are, "Monks and Wandering Friars;" "London in the Middle Ages;" "Gower and Chaucer," etc.

Southey's Early English Naval H.

James's Naval History of England.

Hallam's Constitutional History of England. 4 vols., 8vo. An able, acute, and wonderfully impartial production; indispensable to every thorough student.

Heeren's Political Treatises. Touching the Reformation; Continental interests of Great Britain, etc.

The student may also peruse appropriate biographies, memoirs, travels, Shakespeare's historical plays, Scott's "Ivanhoe," "Kenilworth," and "Fortunes of Nigel." All admirable specimens of the historical novel. Bulwer's "Harold," and "Last of the Barons." Thackeray's "Henry Esmond."

IRELAND.

Moore's (T.) History of Ireland. † Taylor's (W. C.) History of Ireland.

Supplemental List.

Leland's. From the invasion of Henry II. to 1688. Trustworthy.

Thomas D'Arcy McGhee's History of Ireland.

Illustrative Authorities.

* Beaumont's (G. de) Ireland. Social, Political, and Religious. 2 vols.

Goldwin Smith's Irish History, and Irish Church. Displays considerable fairness of judgment and historical acuteness.

* Lieutenant-Colonel Jervis's Ireland under British Rule.

† Trench's Realities of Irish Life. An animated and seemingly honest statement of long experience as estate agent in Ireland. Published in 1869.

Lives of Curran, Grattan, Lord Edward Fitzgerald, Lord Charlemont, etc.

Memoirs of Sir Jonah Barrington.

SCOTLAND.

† Scott's (Sir Walter) Tales of a Grandfather. First three series. Very interesting and spirited

Supplemental List.

Laing's.

Tytler's. 4 vols. Full and conscientious.

Burton's. 6 vols. Not yet completed. This is the latest and best History of Scotland.

Illustrative Authorities.

Mignet's History of Mary, Queen of Scots. From the French. Deeply interesting. Bell, McLeod, and Abbott, have written popular lives of Mary, with varying conclusions. In fact, the literature on this subject embraces not far from a thousand volumes.

Dr. W. Robertson's History of Scotland during the Reign of Mary, and part of James VI.

Gilbert Stuart's History of the same period. Stuart and Robertson take opposite views of the character of Mary. Prof. Smyth, in his lectures, commends Stuart's trustworthiness.

Chambers's History of the Rebellion in Scotland.

Miss Strickland's Lives of the Scottish Queens. 8 vols.

The Lives of Wallace, Bruce, Montrose, etc., etc.

The novels "Waverley," "Abbot," "Monastery," etc.

FRANCE.

† "The Student's France." 1 vol., large 12mo. From earliest times to 1852.

Martin's History of France. 4 vols. From the French. "The most serviceable and valuable history of the nation."—*North American Review.* Has reached the fourth edition, and gained prizes on three occasions.

Supplemental List.

D'Anquetil's. Recommended by Prof. W. Smyth and Enc. Britannica.

Michelet's. The production of a brilliant and versatile writer, but vicious in style, and given to romance.

Illustrative Authorities.

G. P. R. James's H. of Charlemagne.

Froissart's Chronicles of England, France, Spain, etc. 2 vols., 8vo. Illuminated. A minute and garrulous, but vivid and romantic chronicle of the fourteeth century by a contemporary.

* Wraxall's Memoirs of the House of Valois (1327–1589). Recommended by Prof. W. Smyth.

Kirk's History of Charles the Bold, Duke of Burgundy. 3 vols. By a young American historian.

Miss Pardoe's Francis I.; his Court and Reign.

James's Life of Henry IV., King of France and Navarre. 2 vols.

Miss Pardoe's Louis XIV., and the Court of France in the Seventeenth Century. 2 vols.

* Voltaire's Age of Louis XIV. A celebrated work of high character.

Thiers's History of the French Revolution. 4 vols., 8vo. From the French. The eminence of Thiers as an historian is universally acknowledged. He is, however, occasionally prejudiced. Thiers is an advocate of constitutional monarchy.

† Mignet, the same.

Carlyle's French Revolution. 3 vols.

* Von Sybel's History of Europe during the French Revolution. 4 vols. From the German. Just completed.

Edmund Burke's Letter on the same. Created a great sensation. Burke was opposed to the Revolution.

Sir James Mackintosh's Reply to last. Greatly admired. Sir J. modified his opinions subsequently.

Lamartine's History of the Girondists. Has great beauty of style.

De Tocqueville's Old Régime and the French Revolution. An author of great weight.

Thiers's History of the Consulate and Empire. 4 vols., 8vo.

Prof. W. Smyth's Lectures on the French Revolution. Excellent.

Ségur's Napoleon's Expedition to Russia in 1812.

Sir R. Wilson's Narrative of the Invasion of Russia by Napoleon. Very trustworthy. Sir R. W. was with the Russians the entire period.

Louis Blanc's History of Ten Years. 2 vols., 8vo, 1830–1840. The most brilliant, most labored, and most exact of all. Louis Blanc is an ardent republican.

Sir James Stephen's Lectures on the History of France. Very brilliant.

See also "Memoirs" (in which the French excel); "Lives;" "Travels," under the respective heads. Sir W. Scott's "Quentin Durward;" Bulwer's "Richelieu" (drama); De Vigny's "Cinq-Mars;" Mühlbach's novels, etc.

ITALY AND SWITZERLAND.

Spalding's (W.) History of Italy and the Italian Islands. 3 vols., 18mo. A standard work.

Percival's (Geo.) History of Italy. 2 vols.

Napier's (Sir W.) Florentine History. Remarkable for research, copiousness, and elegance.

Sismondi's (J. C. L.) History of the Italian Republics. 1 vol. A useful abridgment of a great work.

Zschokke's (H.) History of Switzerland. A popular history, with continuation to 1848 by Zschokke's son.

Illustrative Authorities.

L. Ranke's History of the Popes in the Sixteenth and Seventeenth Centuries. 3 vols., 8vo. Busk has written the Lives of the Mediæval Popes, and Cardinal Wiseman of the last four.

Flagg's Venice; the City of the Sea.

G. W. Greene's Historical Studies.

DENMARK, SWEDEN, NORWAY.

* Crichton and Wheaton's History of Denmark, Sweden, and Norway. 2 vols., 18mo. Gives the early and modern history, with an account of their government, laws, etc.

Sindig's (P. C.) History of Scandinavia. By a native historian. Dunham's History is excellent, but rare.

Illustrative Authorities.

Wheaton's History of the Northmen.

Mallet's Northern Antiquities.

Vertot's Revolutions in Sweden. The last two from the French.

Lives of Gustavus Adolphus, Charles XII., etc.

RUSSIA, POLAND, HUNGARY.

* Kelly's (W. K.) History of Russia. 2 vols. An able compilation from Karamsin, Tooke, Ségur, etc.

Fletcher's (James) History of Poland. Or, Van Zandt's. Dunham's History of Poland is perhaps the best, but rare.

Anonymous. * Hungary and its Revolutions. Published by Bohn, London.

Illustrative Authorities.

Schnitzler's Secret History of the Court of Russia.

Mackintosh's Essay on the Partitions of Poland. A luminous *exposé*. To be seen in the volume of his collected essays.

Miss Pardoe's City of the Magyars.

Winkstein's History of the War in 1848–'49.

Life of Peter the Great.

* Smucker's Memoirs of Catharine II.

NETHERLANDS, HOLLAND.

* Grattan's (T. C.) H. of the Netherlands. To the Revolution of 1830.

Motley's (J. L.) Rise of the Dutch Republic. 3 vols., 8vo. Brilliant and luxuriant in style, vivid in description, but the work of a vehement partisan. From 1555 to 1584.

Motley's (J. L.) History of the United Netherlands. 4 vols., 8vo. Embracing the period from the death of William the Silent to the Synod of Dort, 1584–1618. A valuable work, but scarcely equal to the former in power, and more tinged with the author's political views.

GERMANY, AUSTRIA, PRUSSIA.

Kohlrausch's (F.) History of Germany. 8vo. From earliest times to peace of 1815. Or, Menzel's History of Germany.

Coxe's (Archdeacon) History of the House of Austria. 4 vols. From Rudolph of Hapsburg to Leopold II., 1218–1792. Bohn has published a new and revised edition, bringing down to the present time.

* "M. A. D.'s" History of Prussia. Small 12mo. From Frederick I., the first king, to 1867.

Illustrative Authorities.

Dr. Robertson's History of the Reign of the Emperor Charles V., with additions by W. H. Prescott. 3 vols., 8vo. The most valuable work of an acute historian.

Carlyle's Life of Frederick the Great. 6 vols. There is no history of this stirring period to compare with Carlyle's.

Hozier's Seven Weeks' War. 2 vols. A graphic and impartial account of the late (1866) war between Prussia and Austria.

SPAIN, AND PORTUGAL.

* Calcott's (Mrs.) History of Spain. Recommended by Smyth in his Lectures.

Dunham's History of Spain and Portugal.

Illustrative Authorities.

Florian's Moors in Spain.

Southey's Chronicle of the Cid.

Washington Irving's Conquest of Granada. A most interesting episode in Spanish history, narrated in a manner truly captivating.

W. Irving's Alhambra.

Florian's Life of Gonsalvo of Cordova. Spain's greatest general.

W. H. Prescott's History of the Reign of Ferdinand and Isabella. 3 vols. Prescott's well-known merits and beauties as an historian render any notice unnecessary.

Robertson's History of the Emperor Charles V. 3 vols. Edited by Prescott. A standard classic.

W. H. Prescott's History of the Reign of Philip II. 3 vols.

Ford's The Spaniards and their Country. No better authority on Spain than Ford.

Napier's Peninsular War. 5 vols., 8vo. Unsurpassed of its kind.

GREECE, TURKEY.

* Finlay's (G.) History of Greece. Published in four distinct works, viz., "Under the Romans from 146 B. C. to 717 A. D.;" "From its Conquest by the Crusaders to its Conquest by the Turks, 1204–1461;" "The History of the Byzantine and Greek Emperors, 716–1453;" "History of Greece under the Ottoman and Venetian Dominion." Finlay has also written an account of the Greek Revolution.

Baird's (Rev. H.) Modern Greece.

Lamartine's (A.) History of Turkey. 3 vols.

Creasy's (Prof.) History of the Ottoman Empire.

ASIA—ARABIA, CHINA, JAPAN, JAVA.

* Crighton's (Rev. A.) History of Arabia. Ancient and modern. 2 vols., 18mo. Describes the country, inhabitants, institutions, and antiquities.

Davis's (J. T.) History of China. 2 vols. Excellent authority.

"Siebold's (Ph. von)" Japan and the Japanese in the Nineteenth Century.

* Raffles's (Sir T. J.) History of Java. 2 vols. A very interesting and authentic account.

INDIA, CABUL, Etc.

Allen's (D. O.) India, Ancient and Modern. Dr. Allen was an American missionary for many years, and in his useful work gives late and full information upon India, social, political, and historical.

* Marshman's (J. C.) History of India from the Earliest Times to the Close of Lord Dalhousie's Administration. 3 vols. The latest and best.

* Bohn's India, Pictorial, Descriptive, and Historical. A good and popular history in small compass.

Supplemental List.

* Malcolm's History of British India. "Has become the manual of modern Indian diplomacy."

* Montgomery Martin's Works.

Murray, Wilson's, etc., British India. 3 vols. A full historic and descriptive account.

Miss Martineau's British Rule in India. An acute *exposé* of abuses.

* Mountstuart Elphinstone's Account of the Kingdom of Cabul, with its Dependencies in Tartary, Persia, and India.

Thornton's History of India.

See also Lives of Clive, Hastings, Lawrence, etc., and "Travels."

AFRICA—EGYPT, BARBARY STATES, Etc.

* Russell's (M.) History of Egypt. A succinct account of ancient and modern Egypt. Or, see Sharpe's History.

* Russell's (M.) History of the Barbary States. See "Travels" for further account of Africa generally.

Ellis's (Rev. W.) Three Visits to Madagascar, 1853–'56.

See also * G. W. Cooke's Conquest and Civilization in North Africa. An excellent survey of French rule and prospects.

Pulsky's Tricolor on the Atlas.

Ditson's Crescent and French Crusaders. Any one of the last three works would afford all needed information.

UNITED STATES—CANADA.

† Quackenbos's History of the United States. A good and late elementary work. Goodrich, Frost, Miss Willard, McDonald, and Blackburn, etc., have written compendious histories.

† Bancroft's (G.) History of the United States. 9 vols., 8vo. The tenth and last volume is in preparation. Although marked occasionally by a partisan spirit, destined to be the standard history of the nation.

McMullen's (J.) History of Canada. 1 vol., large 8vo. From the first discovery to 1867.

* Grahame's (Jas.) History of North America. 4 vols., 8vo. An able and impartial account from a European point of view.

Supplemental List.

Hildreth's History of the United States. 6 vols. Extends only to President Monroe's second term of office.

Murray's Historical Account of British America. 2 vols.

Tucker's History of the United States.

Illustrative Authorities.

EARLY HISTORY.

Smith's (J. Toulmin) Discovery of America by the Northmen, in the Tenth Century.

Robertson's (Dr. W.) History of America; its Discovery and Settlement.

* Helps's (Arthur) Spanish Conquest in America. 4 vols. All three works of high repute.

† Parkman's (F.) History of Pontiac. Pioneers of France in the New World.

Palfrey's (J. H.) History of New England during the Stuart Dynasty.

Schaick's Life of Peter von Schaick.

REVOLUTIONARY WAR.

Botta's History of the War of Independence. Correct and impartial. Botta was an Italian.

† Lee's (Gen. Henry) Memoirs of the War in the Southern Department of the United States. There is a new edition by Gen. R. E. Lee. "As fascinating as a romance, though they undoubtedly contain true history."—*Kent.*

Tarleton's (Lieutenant-Colonel) History of the Campaigns of 1780–'81 in the Southern Provinces of North America. An English account.

Campbell's (W. W.) Annals of Tryon County; or, Border Warfare of New York.

Lossing's (B. J.) Field-Book of the Revolution. 2 vols., 8vo. With plans, cuts, etc.

WAR OF 1812.

Armstrong's (J.) Notices of the War of 1812. 2 vols. Thoroughly honest.

Ingersoll's (C. J.) Second War between the United States and Great Britain. 3 vols.

Lossing's (B. J.) History of the War of 1812. The latest work.

WAR WITH MEXICO.

Ripley's (R. S.) War with Mexico. 2 vols. Or,

Brooks's (N. C.). The same.

CIVIL WAR.

Draper's (J. W.) History of the American Civil War. 3 vols. Not yet completed.

Greeley's (Horace) American Conflict. 2 vols., 8vo.

Stephens's (Alex. H.) History of the War between the States. 1 vol. published. Chiefly political in character.

Pollard's (E. A.) Lost Cause.

Swinton's Campaigns of the Army of the Potomac.

Swinton's Decisive Battles of the War.

Semmes's (Admiral) Memoirs of Service Afloat during the War between the States.

Harper's (publishers) Pictorial History of the Great Rebellion. 2 vols., 4to.

Boynton's (Rev. C. B.) History of the American Navy during the Great Rebellion. 2 vols.

Appletons' (publishers) Naval and Military History of the Rebellion. 1 vol., 8vo.

Dabney's (Rev. Dr.) Life of Stonewall Jackson. Or, by J. E. Cooke.

N. B.—For reference, Frank Moore's "Rebellion Record" is very useful. For Histories of the individual States, see Appendix under the head "Library," where additional works on American history may be seen. See also Lives, Memoirs, and the historical novels of Cooper, Kennedy, and Simms. Also Elliott's Debates.

MEXICO, CENTRAL AMERICA.

† Prescott's (W. H.) Conquest of Mexico. 3 vols., 8vo. A history vying with any romance in the fascination of its story, and abounding in curious and valuable information.

Diaz (Bernal). True History of the Conquest of Mexico. There is a great charm in this *naive* record. Diaz was one of Cortez's captains.

* Wilson's (R. A.) Mexico. Assails the prevalent account of the conquest by Cortez.

Squier's (E. G.) Central America. A description of the country, people, and institutions.

SOUTH AMERICA, WEST INDIES.

† Prescott's (W. H.) Conquest of Peru. 3 vols., 8vo. Most instructive, and of absorbing interest.

Kidder and Fletcher's History of Brazil. 8vo. Eighth edition. Contains the latest information, and fairly exhausts the subject.

King's (J. A.) Twenty-four Years in the Argentine Republic.

Holton's New Granada.

Hassaurek's Four Years in Spanish America (1861–'65). Hassaurek's official position in Equador furnished a good opportunity for collecting information.

* Edwards's History of the West Indies.

Supplemental List.

* Southey's History of Brazil. Long favorably known.

Helps's Spanish Conquest in America. A late and standard work.

Grimshaw's History of South America. 12mo. There is also a brief historical sketch in Goodrich's History of America.

See also, "Travels."

OCEANICA.

Russell's (M.) History of Polynesia. Includes the chief islands in the Pacific, and New Zealand.

Horne's (R. H.) Australian Facts and Prospects. Entertaining and instructive. Mr. Horne spent seven years in Australia.

Anonymous. Australia. Published by Pott & Amery, New York.

Thompson's (D. A.) The Story of New Zealand, Past and Present. The latest and best authority.

Jarves's (J. J.) History of the Hawaiian or Sandwich Islands. There is a later English account by H. Manley.

GENERAL HISTORY—Modern.

† Taylor's (W. C.) Manual of Modern History. A capital elementary book. Or,

Michelet's Elements of the Modern History of Europe. From the French.

White's Eighteen Christian Centuries. Highly interesting.

Heeren's Political System of Europe and its Colonies. 2 vols. Admirable.

Alison's (Sir A.) History of Europe, from the Fall of Napoleon (1815) to the Accession of Louis Napoleon (1852). 2 vols., 8vo.

Alison's (Sir A.) History of Europe from 1789 to 1815. 10 vols., 8vo.
" " " " " 1852 to 1860–'61.

The last three works form a vast storehouse of facts; but the judgment of the author is not always equal to his industry. There is an abridged edition of this series.

Supplemental List.

Tytler's Universal History. 6 vols.

Von Müller's Universal History.

W. Russell's History of Modern Europe.

* Von Sybel's History of Europe during the French Revolution. 4 vols. Now (1870) completed.

SPECIAL HISTORY (pertaining to History Proper).

* Wheaton's History of the Northmen.

Palgrave's History of the Anglo-Saxons. For a minute account, Turner can be consulted.

Ockley's History of the Saracens. "A faithful and interesting account."

Ranke's History of the Popes in the Sixteenth and Seventeenth Centuries.

Gervinus's Introduction to the History of the Nineteenth Century. From the German. Distinguished by its liberal sentiments.

† Creasy's Fifteen Decisive Battles of the World. A very pleasant and instructive book.

Vertot's Achievements of the Knights of Malta. Rather romantic.

Knight's "Weekly Volume" Series—Historic Parallels.

Delepierre's Historical Difficulties and Contested Events. Discusses the stories of Belisarius, Pope Joan, Abeilard, Eloisa, and William Tell, etc.; also the alleged discoveries of inventors.

Catlin's (George) Letters on the Manners, Customs, and Condition, of the North American Indians. 2 vols., 8vo. See also Schoolcraft.

MISCELLANEOUS HISTORY (*not* CONSTITUTING HISTORY PROPER).

ECCLESIASTICAL.

Stanley's (Dean) Lectures on the History of the Jewish Church. 2 vols., 8vo. In two parts, from Abraham to Samuel, and from Samuel to the Captivity.

Stanley's (Dean) Lectures on History of the Eastern Church. 1 vol., 8vo.
" " Sinai and Palestine. All three works of the highest order.

Merivale's (Ch.) Conversion of the Roman Empire. 1 vol., large 12mo.
" " " Northern Nations. 1 vol., large 12mo.
Both of high repute.

Gieseler's (Dr. J. C.) Ecclesiastical History. Fifth volume published. The merits of this work are acknowledged on all sides. Dr. Schaff's "Ecclesiastical History" is also excellent. Mosheim is rather antiquated. See also Wiltsch's "Hand-book of Church Geography," etc.

D'Aubigné's History of the Reformation. 5 vols. Archbishop Spalding, in his History, gives the Roman Catholic views.

Neal's (D.) History of the Puritans. 2 vols.

Smiles's Huguenots. Relating to England and Ireland, and partly to America.

Supplemental List.

* Dean Milman's History of Christianity, etc. 3 vols. "From the Birth of Christ to the Abolition of Paganism in the Roman Empire."

* Dean Milman's History of Latin Christianity. 9 vols. Both works exhibit admirable learning and impartiality.

McCrie's History of the Reformation in Scotland.

Steinmetz's History of the Jesuits. Nicolini's is also good.

Chateaubriand's Martyrs. J. H. Newman's Callista, and Cardinal Wiseman's Fabiola, are works of fiction, which afford interesting pictures of early Christian times.

VARIOUS HISTORICAL SUBJECTS.

Mill's History of Chivalry.

James's (G. P. R.) History of the Secret Societies of the Middle Ages.

Llorente's (J. A.) History of the Inquisition. 2 vols., 8vo.

† Baring-Gould's Curious Myths of the Middle Ages. Two series. Treats of the Wandering Jew, Prester John, the Divining Rod, etc.

Brinton's (D. G.) Myths of the New World.

† Guizot's History of Civilization in Europe. 3 vols. A standard work. There is an abridgment.

* Lubbock's (Sir J.) Prehistoric Times, etc. "As Illustrated by Ancient Remains, and the Manners and Customs of Modern Savages." A valuable work, displaying great research. The edition of 1869 has important additions, narrating some late and singular archæological discoveries.

Argyle's (Duke of) Primeval Man. A short treatise, differing, at times, from both Lubbock and Whately.

* Wilson's (Dr.) Prehistoric Man: being Researches into the Origin of Civilization.

LECTURES, Etc., ON HISTORY.

Niebuhr's Lectures on Ancient History.

Schlegel's " Modern "

Arnold's " " "

† Smyth's (W.) Lectures on Modern History.

Smith's (Goldwin) Lectures on Modern History.

Bolingbroke's (Lord) Letters on the Use and Study of History.

Voltaire's Essay on the Manner and Spirit of Nations.

Hegel's Philosophy of History.

Smith's (Goldwin) On the Study of History.

† Stephen's (Sir James) Lectures on the History of France.

II.—BIOGRAPHY.

BIOGRAPHY is, in some respects, the essence of all other reading. In the lives of eminent men we find the key to history, the dawning and the development of science, the progress of art and philosophy, and the effects of religion. It is naturally one of the most interesting as well as one of the most instructive branches of study. I have, therefore, not hesitated to give a long list under this head, and yet some celebrated names will be found omitted. To explain this, it must be borne in mind that not a few great men are without worthy biographies; others have led lives of which the main importance consisted in the development of their own minds, of which no record could be obtained; and, again, of some great men we know next to nothing.

ANCIENT.

Grote's (George) Life of Socrates (Greek philosopher), B. C. 470–400. Full title, "Life and Teachings of Socrates."

Williams's (Rev. J.) Life of Alexander the Great, B. C. 356–323.

Arnold's (Th.) Life of Hannibal (Carthaginian general), B. C. 247–183.

Forsyth's Life of Cicero (Roman orator, etc.), B. C. 106–43.

Napoleon's (Louis) Life of Cæsar, Julius (Roman general, etc.), B. C. 100–44. Or by H. G. Liddell.

* Mahon's (Lord) Life of Belisarius (Roman general), A. D. –565. "This story will never lose its interest. Mahon adheres to the old version, in spite of Gibbon."—*Charles King.*

† "Plutarch's Lives." 5 vols., 8vo. Embracing forty-six Greeks and Romans. Best edition by A. E. Clough. There is an abridgment.

† Irving's (Washington) Life of Mohammed, 569–622. 2 vols. Includes his "Successors." Muir, Bush, and Gibbon, have also written Lives of

Mohammed. Muir's is considered the best. The latest is a small volume with notes by Milman, etc.

ENGLISH, IRISH, SCOTTISH.

Asser's Life of Alfred the Great, 849–900. Asser was the tutor and friend of Alfred. There are also recent and interesting Lives of Alfred by Dr. Pauli and Thomas Hughes.

Milman's (Dean) Life of À Becket, Thomas (Archbishop of Canterbury), –1170.

McCrie's Life of Knox, Jno. (Scottish reformer), 1505–'72.

McFarland's Life of Gresham, Sir Thomas (celebrated merchant), 1517–'79. Or, Life by C. Knight.

Bell's Life of Mary, Queen of Scotts, 1542–'87. Also by Mignet, Abbott, McLeod, etc., etc.

Barrow's (Sir J.) Life of Drake, Admiral, 1545–'96. With "Voyages." Best edition, second, abridged.

St. John's (J. A.) Life of Raleigh, Sir Walter, 1552–1618. Or by Charles Kingsley, or Ed. Edwards, 1869.

Dixon's (Hepworth) Life of Bacon, Lord, (philosopher, writer, etc.), 1552–1618. Full title, "Personal History of," etc. There is a recent French Life by Ch. Remusat; one by Basil Montagu, in his edition of Bacon's works; and by others. Macaulay, in his "Essays," gives a sketch of Bacon's life, with a review of the controverted points.

White's (R. Grant) Life of Shakespeare, William, 1564–1616. Full title, "Life and Genius of," etc. There is also a good Life by C. Knight, and a biographical sketch by Guizot; not to specify many others.

* Forster's (Jno.) Life of Eliot, Sir John (patriot and statesman), 1590–1632. An admirable and instructive narrative.

Nugent's (Lord) Life of Hampden, Jno. (patriot and statesman), 1594–1643.

† Forster's (Jno.) Life of Cromwell, Oliver (patriot and statesman), 1599–1658. A splendid piece of biography.

Carlyle's (Thomas) Letters, etc., of Cromwell, Oliver (patriot and statesman), 1599–1658. With a connecting sketch of the life. See also Life by J. R. Andrews, just published, and hostile to Cromwell.

Dixon's (Hepworth) Life of Blake, Admiral, 1599–1661.

"Autobiography of Hutchinson, Mrs., 1619–. Gives a lifelike picture of the times during the Civil War.

* Keightley's (Thomas) Life of Milton, John (the poet, etc.), 1608–'74. The best Life out, take it all in all. Contains a useful account of Milton's writings, and an introduction to Paradise Lost. A good short

Life is Masson's—*not* his large biography—with an "Estimate of the Genius and Character of Milton," by Macaulay.

Guizot's Life of Monk, General, 1608–'70. An historical study more than a "Life."

Brewster's (Sir David) Life of Newton, Sir Isaac (mathematician, etc.).

Dixon's (Hep.) Life of Penn, William, 1644–1718. The edition of 1856 contains an answer to Macaulay's charges. J. Paget, of Edinburgh, has also answered Macaulay's strictures. There is also a good Life by Janney, an American author.

Coxe's (Archdeacon) Life of Marlborough, Duke of (general), 1650–1722. Or by Alison; or, in Gleig's Lives of Commanders.

Aikin's (Lucy) Life of Addison, Joseph (poet, essayist, etc.), 1672–1719. Or, by Macaulay, in Essays.

† Southey's (Robert) Life of Wesley, Rev. John, 1703–'91. Written with great beauty of style.

† Macaulay's Life of Chatham, Lord (orator, etc.), 1708–'78. See Macaulay's "Essays."

† Boswell's Life of Johnson, Dr. Samuel (author), 1709–'84. Perhaps the most popular biography ever written. Croker's edition—though containing not a few errors—the best.

Autobiography of Hume, David (historian and philosopher), 1711–'76.

Fitzgerald's (Percy) Life of Garrick, David (actor, etc.), 1716–'79. Very interesting.

Leslie's (Charles) Life of Reynolds, Sir Joshua (painter), 1723–'92. Edited by Tom Taylor. Or, Life by Northcote.

Gleig's (Rev. G. R.) Life of Clive, Lord (Indian statesman, etc.), 1725–'85. † Or, see brilliant sketch in Macaulay's Essays.

Dixon's (Hep.) Life of Howard, John (philanthropist), 1726–'90. Edition of 1854.

* Prior's (Jas.) Life of Burke, Edmund (orator, etc.), 1730–'97. A standard classic.

* † Irving's (Washington) Life of Goldsmith, Oliver (poet, etc.), 1731–'74. Or by Forster; or Prior.

Gleig's (Rev. G. R.) Life of Hastings, Warren (Indian statesman, etc.), 1733–1818. † Or in Macaulay's Essays.

* Smiles's (Samuel) Life of Watt, James (engineer, etc.), 1736–1819. Or by Muirhead.

Autobiography of Gibbon, Edward (historian), 1737–'94. There is a Life by Lord Sheffield.

Jewett's (L.) Lives of Wedgwoods, the (potters), 1739, etc. 1 vol., 8vo. Or, by Miss Meteyard. 2 vols., 8vo.

Knowles's (John) Life of Fuseli (a Swiss painter), 1739–1825. 3 vols. Enriched by valuable criticisms on art, etc.

Hazlitt's (William) Life of Northcote (painter), 1746–1831. Abounds in anecdote.

Russell's (Earl) Life of Fox, C. James (orator and statesman), 1748–1806.

Bowring's (Sir John) Life of Bentham, Jeremy (publicist), 1749–1832.

Wilberforce's (R. and S.) Life of Wilberforce, William (philanthropist, etc.), 1750–1830. * Condensed edition, Murray, 1868.

Phillips's (Charles) Life of Curran, J. Philpot (orator, etc.), 1750–1817. Title, "Curran and his Contemporaries."

Grattan's (H.) Life of Grattan, Henry (patriot and orator), 1750–1820. 5 vols.

* Moore's (Thomas) Life of Sheridan, R. B. (orator and dramatist), 1751–1816. 2 vols. A standard biography. [2 vols.

* Campbell's (Th.) Life of Siddons, Mrs. (celebrated actress), 1755–1831.

Autobiography of Gifford, William (critic), 1756–1826.

" Romilly, Sir Samuel (lawyer), 1757–1818. 2 vols. Edited by his sons, with a selection of his correspondence.

* † Southey's Life of Nelson, Lord (naval commander), 1758–1805. A model of prose composition.

Macaulay's (Lord) Life of Pitt, William (statesman) 1759–1806. Or by Earl Stanhope.

Lockhart's (J. G.) Life of Burns, Robert (poet), 1759–'96. Or, by Robert Chambers; Dr. Currie; or Thomas Carlyle.

Autobiography of Leslie, C. R. (painter), 1760–. Edited by Tom Taylor. Very entertaining.

Moore's (Thomas) Life of Fitzgerald, Lord Edward (patriot), 1763–'98. A tragic narrative.

Brialmont's Life of Wellington, Duke of, 1769–1852. 4 vols. The author was a captain on the Belgian staff. The book is not only intrinsically good, but, as the production of a foreigner, is useful to compare with English biographies; of these, Maxwell's and Gleig's are the most popular. Stocquelen's is recommended. The Life by J. Lemoine gives a French view.

* † Lockhart's (J. G.) Life of Scott, Sir Walter, 1771–1832. 7 vols. Admirable in every respect, in taste, judgment, impartiality, and style. Lockhart was son-in-law of Scott.

Campbell's (Lord) Life of Lyndhurst, Lord (lawyer), 1772–1863. Marred by jealous prejudices. In same volume with Life of Brougham.

Barry Cornwall's Life of Lamb, Charles (essayist, etc.), 1775–1834. Or, by Talfourd.

* Forster's (John) Life of Landor, Walter Savage (author), 1775–1864. Excellent, though rather diffuse.

Allen's (J.) Life of Dundonald, Lord (naval commander), 1775–1860. Full of feats of noble daring. There is an extended Life by his son, and a "Narrative" by himself. In early life his title was Lord Cochrane.

* Yates's (Edward) Life of Matthews, Charles (actor), 1776–1835.

Campbell's (Lord) Life of Brougham, Lord (lawyer, author, etc.), 1779–1868. Published together with Life of Lyndhurst.

* Davy's (D.) Life of Davy, Sir Humphrey (chemist), 1778–1829. Or by his brother, Dr. J. Davy.

* Russell's (Earl) Life of Moore, Thomas (poet), 1780–1852.

Hanna's (Rev. Dr.) Life of Chalmers, Thomas (minister of the Gospel, etc.), 1780–1847.

* Napier's (Major-General W.) Life of Napier, Sir Charles James (military commander, etc.), 1782–1853. A career marked by varied genius and undaunted courage. Sir William, author of History of Peninsular War, and of this biography, was brother of Sir Charles James, and Admiral Sir Charles, their cousin.

* Autobiography of Hunt, Leigh (poet, etc., etc.), 1784–1859. New edition of 1860. "Rich in anecdote, historical, and personal, in description, and in criticism."—*Westminster Review.*

Buxton's (C.) Life of Buxton, Sir Thomas (philanthropist), 1786–1845.

L'Estrange's (Rev. A. G. K.) Life of Mitford, Miss (author), 1786–1855. 2 vols. 12mo. A delightful book.

Autobiography of Haydon, B. F. (painter), 1786–1846. 2 vols. Edited by Tom Taylor. A painful record of struggling talent. Haydon's notices of distinguished people give interest and value to this book.

Madden's (R.) Life of Blessington, Countess of (author), 1787–1849. "Literary Life and Correspondence."

* Moore's (Thomas) Life of Byron, Lord, 1788–1824. 2 vols. "Letters and Journals of, with Notices of his Life." "Deserves to be classed among the best specimens of English prose which our age has produced." "Of deep and painful interest."—*Macaulay.*

Whately's (Miss) Life of Whately, Archbishop (author), 1789–1864. With correspondence.

Rossetti's (W.) Life of Shelley, Percy Bysshe (poet), 1792–1821.

Tyndall's (J.) Life of Faraday, Michael (chemist), 1794–1867. "As a Discoverer." A new Life, by Prof. Jones, is announced.

Stanley's (A. P.) Life of Arnold, Thomas (author and teacher), 1795–1843. With correspondence.

Headley's Life of Havelock, General, 1795–1857.

* † Smiles's (Samuel) Life of Stephenson, Robert (engineer), 1803–'59.

Taylor's (Tom) Life of Thackeray, W. M. (novelist), 1811–'64. A brief sketch.

* Gaskell's (Mrs.) Life of Brontë, Charlotte (novelist), 1816–'55.

† Hodson's Life of Hodson, Captain. Full title, "Twelve Years of a Soldier's Life in India." Edited by his brother. "A book to make those who read it manlier, more honest, more enduring, more energetic."—*Atlantic Monthly.*

McGilchrist's Lives of Cobden, Palmerston, D'Israeli, and Gladstone (statesmen). 4 vols., small 12mo.

COLLECTIONS OF ENGLISH BIOGRAPHY.

Fuller's (Thomas) Worthies of England and Wales. Abounds in amusing anecdote.

Johnson's (Dr. S.) Lives of the Poets. 3 vols. Begins with Cowley. Biassed in its criticisms. The best edition—and greatly improved—is by Peter Cunningham, 1854.

* Forster's (John) Lives of the Statesmen of the Commonwealth. 5 vols., or, 1 vol., 8vo. A very valuable collection. Embraces Eliot, Strafford, Pym, Hampden, Vane, Marten, and Cromwell. Edition of 1854 the best.

Brougham's (Lord) Lives of Men of Letters and of Science of the Times of George III. 2 vols.

* Brougham's (Lord) Historical Sketches of Statesmen who flourished in the Reign of George III.

* Campbell's (Lord) Lives of the Lord Chancellors. 1 vol.

" " " " Chief Justices. 3 vols., 8vo.

" " Eminent Lawyers.

The works of Lord Campbell—late Chancellor—are interesting and instructive, but occasionally prejudiced when discussing contemporaries.

† Taylor's (W. C.) Modern British Plutarch. Much information in small compass. Extends down to 1840 about.

Cunningham's (Allan) Lives of British Painters. 5 vols., 12mo.

Jeaffreson's Lives of British Novelists. 2 vols., 12mo. Instructive and entertaining sketches, with criticisms.

Kaye's (J. W.) Lives of Indian Officers. Refers to East Indies.

† Smiles's (Samuel) Brief Biographies. Embraces last fifty years, and includes some thirty Lives. All Smiles's works are highly esteemed.

† Smiles's (Samuel) Industrial Biography.

* † Smiles's (Samuel) Self-Help. Sketches of Self-Made Men.

Gilfillan's Literary Portraits. 3 series.

Shiel's (Lalor) Sketches of the Irish Bar.

"Wharton's" (G. and P.) Queens of Society. Wits and Beaux of Society. The "Whartons" wrote under a fictitious name. Their books make pleasant reading.

FRENCH, ITALIAN, SPANISH, AND SOUTH-EUROPEAN.

James's (G. P. R.) Life of Charlemagne (the emperor, warrior, and statesman), 742–814.

Joinville's (De) Life of St. Louis (King Louis IX. of France), 1215–'70. Told with charming naïveté.

Campbell's (T.) Life of Petrarch, Francis (poet), 1304–'74.

* † Michelet's Life of Joan of Arc (patriot, etc.), 1402–'31. Also by Miss Harriet Parr ("Holme Lee").

* † Irving's (Wash.) Life of Columbus, Christopher, 1441–1506. 3 vols., 8vo. Embraces his companions, Balboa, Ponce de Leon, etc., etc.

* Roscoe's (W.) Life of Medici, Lorenzo dei (statesman), 1448–'92. 3 vols. A classic biography.

* † Grimm's Life of Angelo, Michael B. (sculptor), 1474–1563. Full of interesting information, and a production of the highest class of biography. There is a shorter Life, by Duppa, in the same volume with De Quincy's Life of Raphael.

* Roscoe's (W.) Life of Leo X., Pope (patron of art and literature), 1475–1521. 2 vols.

Simms's (W. G.) Life of Bayard, the Chevalier (a model knight), 1476–1524. Or, by E. Walford.

* † Autobiography of Cellini, Benvenuto (sculptor and engraver), 1500–'70. One of the finest works of autobiography in any language. Cellini led a stirring life, and was a favorite of some of the greatest men of the age; of these he has given many interesting anecdotes.

Dyer's (T. H.) Life of Calvin, John (theologian), 1509–'64.

Morley's (Prof.) Life of Palissy, Bernard de (potter), 15?–'90. Well worth reading as a record of artistic genius and heroic patience.

Roscoe's Life of Cervantes, Miguel de (novelist and dramatist), 1547–1616.

† Brewster's (Sir D.) Life of Galileo (astronomer, etc.), 1564–1642. Title, "Martyrs of Science."

James's (G. P. R.) Life of Richelieu (statesman), 1585–1642.

Trench's (R. C.) Life of Calderon (dramatist), 1600–'87. Title, "Life and Genius of." This delightful little book does justice, though late, to a great Spanish name. The translations are well executed, and serve to give some idea of the grace and spirit of Spanish poetry.

Mahon's (Lord) Life of Condé, The Great (military commander), 1621–'86. Written with excellent taste and judgment.

Lomenie's (L. de) Life of Beaumarchais (dramatist), 1732–'99. Title, "Beaumarchais and his Times." Very gossipy, but good to while away an idle hour.

Dumont's Life of Mirabeau (orator and politician), 1749–'91. Title, "Recollections of Mirabeau."

Autobiography of Alfieri (dramatist), 1749–1803. The account of his literary toil is curious.

McHarg's (C. K.) Life of Talleyrand (diplomatist), 1754–1838.

Mack's Life of La Fayette, 1757–1834. There are various lives and memoirs—by Cloquet, Holstein, etc.

Abbotts' (J. and J. S. C.) Life of Josephine, The Empress, 1763–1814.

Luyster's (Miss) Life of Récamier, Madame, 1777–1849. A record of no little beauty and interest. From the French.

Falloux's (Count de) Life of Swetchine, Madame (Russian), 1782–1857. A lady eminent for her piety. From the French.

Lee's (Mrs. R.) Life of Cuvier, Baron (German by birth; naturalist), 1769–1832. Title, "Memoirs of," etc.

Hazlitt's (W.) Life of Bonaparte, Napoleon, 1769–1821. An enthusiastic admirer of Bonaparte.

D'Abrantes' (Duchesse) Life of Bonaparte, Napoleon. Title, "Memoirs of the Emperor Napoleon: his Court and Family."

Bourrienne's Life of Bonaparte, Napoleon. Title, "The Court and Camp of Bonaparte." 4 vols.

O'Meara's Life of Bonaparte, Napoleon. Title, "Napoleon in Exile." See "Reply to 'Napoleon in Exile.'"

Jomini's Life of Bonaparte, Napoleon. Translated by General Halleck; chiefly military in character.

† Lockhart's Life of Bonaparte, Napoleon. Sensible and impartial.

Scott's (Sir W.) Life of Bonaparte, Napoleon. Valuable, and generally fair, though it is the fashion to abuse it.

Channing's (Dr.) Life of Bonaparte, Napoleon.

Autobiography of Béranger (French lyric poet), 1780–1857.

Beaumont's (G. de) Life of De Tocqueville (publicist), 1805–'59. Title, "Memoirs, Letters, and Remains of De Tocqueville."

De la Rive's Life of Cavour, Count (Italian statesman), 1809–'62. Title, "Reminiscences," etc. Italian liberty owes much to Cavour.

GERMAN, DANISH, DUTCH, Etc.—NORTH AND MIDDLE EUROPEAN.

† Bunsen's Life of Luther, 1484–1546. With illustrations by Carlyle and Sir W. Hamilton. Or, Gillette's.

Brewster's (Sir D.) Life of Brahe, Tycho (Danish astronomer) 1546–1601. Title "Martyrs of Science."

Brewster's (Sir D.) Life of Kepler (German astronomer), 1571–1630. In same volume as Brahe's Life.

Heydenreich's (Rev. L.) Life of Gustavus Adolphus (King of Sweden, etc.), 1594–1633. * Chapman's Life is the best.

Palmer's Life of Sobieski (Polish king and hero), 1629–'96.

Mackie's (J.) Life of Leibnitz (German philosopher), 1646–1716.

Barrow's (Sir J.) Life of Peter the Great (Emperor of Russia, etc.), 1672–1725. Or, Voltaire's Life of Peter.

Voltaire's Life of Charles XII. (Swedish warrior), 1682–1718.

Schoelcher's Life of Händel (German composer and performer), 1684–1759.

† Macaulay's (T. B.) Life of Frederick the Great (Prussian king and general), 1712–'86. Short and brilliant.

Carlyle's (Thos.) Life of Frederick the Great (Prussian king and general), 1712–1786. 3 vols., 8vo. Able, impartial, and original in its treatment.

Stahr's (Adolf) Life of Lessing (Prussian author), 1729–'81. "The Life and Works of Lessing." From the German.

Autobiography of "Stilling" (a singular enthusiast), 1740–1817.

Autobiography of Goethe (poet, dramatist, critic, etc.), 1749–1831. Translated by Parke Godwin.

† Lewes's (G. H.) Life of Goethe. Second edition, 1864.

Rau's (E.) Life of Mozart (Austrian composer), 1756–'91. Title, "Biographical Sketch of Mozart."

Carlyle's (Thomas) Life of Schiller (German poet, dramatist, etc.), 1759–1805.

† Klencke and Schlesier's Life of Humboldt, Alexander, 1769–1859. And
" " " William, 1767–1835. Translated and condensed by Juliette Bauer. Or, Life by Stoddart.

Bunsen's Life of Niebuhr (Danish historian), 1776–1830. With Letters—admirable they are.

* Bunsen's (Baroness) Life of Bunsen, Baron (German author, etc.), 1791–1860. Get the condensed edition.

* Grote's (Mrs.) Life of Scheffer, Ary (Dutch painter), 1795–1858.

Liszt's Life of Chopin (Polish composer and musician), 1810–'49.

Lampadius's Life of Mendelssohn (German composer), 1809–'47.

COLLECTIONS of EUROPEAN BIOGRAPHY—omitting BRITISH.

James's (G. P. R.) Lives of Foreign Statesmen. 2 vols., 12mo. Assisted by E. E. Crowe, embracing, among others:

Cardinal d'Amboise.	Ximenes.	De Witt.
Maurice of Saxony.	Leo X.	Necker.
Oxenstiern.	Sully.	Cardinal Alberoni.
Cardinal de Retz.	Mazarin.	Cardinal de Fleury.
Richelieu.	Colbert.	Marquis de Pombal.
	Duke de Choiseul.	

Montgomery's (M.) Life of Authors of Italy, Spain, and Portugal. 2 vols., 12mo. Aided by Sir D. Brewster, etc.

Dante.	Vittoria Colonna.	Cervantes.
Petrarch.	Torquato Tasso.	Calderon.
Boccaccio.	Metastasio.	Lope de Vega.
Ariosto.	Galileo.	Camoëns.
Bojardo.	Filicaja.	Garcilaso de Vega.
Machiavelli.	Goldoni.	Ugo Foscolo.
Guicciardini.	Alfieri.	etc., etc.

Shelley's (Mrs.) Lives of Authors of France. 2 vols., 12mo. Embracing, among others:

Montaigne.	La Fontaine.	Fénelon.
Rabelais.	Pascal.	Voltaire.
Corneille.	Racine.	Rousseau.
Rochefoucauld.	Sévigné.	Condorcet.
Molière.	Boileau.	Mirabeau.
	Madame Roland.	

N. B.—The above series belong to the Edinburgh Cabinet Library. Lea & Blanchard published an abridgment of James's Lives.

Walsh's (R. M.) "Sketches of Conspicuous Living Characters of France." Lea & Blanchard, 1841.

Jameson's (Mrs.) Lives of the Italian Painters. Greatly esteemed. Best edition, 1868.

AMERICAN.

† Hillard's (G. S.) Life of Smith, Captain John, 15 –1631. Or by W. G. Simms.

† Autobiography of Franklin, Benjamin, 1706–'90. Edited by Godwin, or Bigelow.

Sparks's Life of Franklin, Benjamin. Or, by Parton.

Irving's (Washington) Life of Washington, 1732–'99. 5 vols. Or, by Marshall, Sparks, Ramsay, † Everett, Guizot.

Simms's (W. G.) Life of Marion, General, 17 –'95.

Adams's (C. F.) Life of Adams, John, 1735–1826.
Wirt's " Henry, Patrick, 1736–'99.
Mackenzie's (Captain S.) Life of Jones, Paul, 1736–'92.
Caldwell's Life of Greene, General N., 1742–'86.
† Autobiography of Jefferson, Thomas, 1743–1826.
Tucker's Life of Jefferson, Thomas. Or, by Randall, his grandson. There are various other biographies.
Jay's Life of Jay, John, 1745–1829. Or, by Renwick.
Redpath's (J.) Life of Toussaint, L'Ouverture, 1745–1803.
Rives's " Madison, James, 1751–1836.
Diary, etc., of Lawrence, Amos, 1755–1852. Title, "Extracts from the Diary and Correspondence of."
Parton's Life of Burr, Aaron, 1756–1836. Or, by M. L. Davis.
† Renwick's " Hamilton, Alexander, 1757–1804. Or, by his son.
Colden's (C. D.) Life of Fulton, Robert, 1767–1815.
† Parton's " Jackson, Andrew, 1767–1845.
Hoosack's " Clinton, De Witt, 1769–1828. Or, by Renwick.
Kennedy's (J. P.) " Wirt, William, 1772–1835.
Garland's " Randolph, John, 1773–1833.
Colton's (Calvin) " Clay, Henry, 1777–1852. With speeches.
Channing's (W. H.) " Channing, W. E., 1780–1842.
† Curtis's (G. T.) " Webster, Daniel, 1782–1852.
Irving's (P. M.) " Irving, Washington, 1783–1859. 4 vols., 12mo.
Mackenzie's (Captain S.) Life of Perry, Commodore O. H., 1785–1820.
Mansfield's " Scott, Major-General Winfield, 1786–1866. Or, by Headley.
Ticknor's Life of Prescott, W. H., 1796–1859.
Hassard's (J. R.) Life of Hughes, Archbishop, 1798–1864.
Brown's (Prof. S. G.) Life of Choate, Rufus, 1799–1850.
Emerson's (R. W., etc.) Life of Fuller, Margaret, 1810–'50.

COLLECTIONS OF AMERICAN BIOGRAPHY.

† Belknap's American Biography. 3 vols., 18mo.
Sparks's Library of American Biography. Two series. 25 vols.
† Ellet's (Mrs.) Women of the American Revolution.
† Cooper's (J. F.) Lives of Distinguished American Naval Officers. 2 vols., 12mo.
Sprague's American Pulpit. Embraces Episcopalians, Presbyterians, etc., etc. Entertaining as well as instructive.
Flanders's Lives of the Chief Justices of the Supreme Court.

Hunt's (Freeman) Lives of American Merchants.

Tuckerman's Book of the Artists. American Artist Life.

Davidson's (Prof.) Living Writers of the South. Published December, 1869. Full, but neither complete nor discriminative.

COLLECTIONS OF MISCELLANEOUS BIOGRAPHY.

† Arago's Biographies of Distinguished Scientific Men. Two series. Translated, with corrections, by Admiral Smith and Rev. Baden Powell. A delightful series. See also Fontenelle's Éloges.

† Craik's (G. L.) Pursuit of Knowledge under Difficulties. Two series.

Smiles's (Samuel) Brief Biographies. Industrial Biography. Self-Help. The last work is illustrated by examples.

† Smiles's (Samuel) Lives of the Engineers. Embracing Smeaton, Brindley, Telford, etc., etc.

† Smiles's (Samuel) Lives of George and Robert Stephenson.

Howe's (H.) Lives of Eminent Mechanics. Embracing Fitch, Whitney, Eckford, etc., etc.

Spooner's Biographical Dictionary of Painters, etc. Or, Dr. Shepherd's abridgment of Pilkington.

Mitchell's (General) Biography of Eminent Soldiers of the last Four Centuries.

Timbs's (J.) Inventors and Discoverers.

Edwards's (B. B.) Biography of Self-Taught Men.

Seymour's (C. B.) Self-Made Men.

Ellett's (Mrs.) Women Artists in All Ages.

Crossland's (Mrs.) Memorable Women, and the Stories of their Lives. Comprising Lady Sale, Lady Russell, etc.

Balfour's (Clara L.) Working Women of the Last Century. Hannah More, Charlotte Elizabeth, etc.

* Trotter's (Captain) Studies in Biography. Concise, and showing good judgment.

Burney's (Admiral) History of the Buccaneers in the South Sea, up to George III.

Abbotts' (J. and J. S. C.) Illustrated Biographies. A favorite series with young folks.

Thatcher's Indian Biography.

* Gronow's (Captain) Celebrities of London and Paris. Fourth series, 1867. Full of entertainment and instruction.

III.—TRAVELS.

BOOKS of travel, like biography, combine, in a marked degree, the useful and the agreeable. Next to actual travelling, they enlarge our ideas respecting our fellow-men, and correct national prejudices. I have taken much pains, not only to arrange the works cited below in chronological order, but also to make such a selection—as far as this was practicable—as would enable the reader to get descriptions of the same country by travellers of different nationalities, and at different times. With this object, I have sought diligently foreign books of travel of repute, when to be found in English dress. To read works of travel with profit, constant reference should be made to the map.

The letter (p.) after a date denotes the time of publication in the United States.

EUROPE.

England, 1670 (about), * Cosmo III., Travels through. Cosmo was a Grand-duke of Tuscany.

Hebrides, 1773, Boswell's Journal of a Tour to the. In company with Dr. Johnson.

Great Britain, 1831–'35, Colton's Four Years' Residence in.

" 1832, Allen's Practical Tourist. Abounds in useful information.—*Kent.*

" 1837, p. Howitt's Visits to Remarkable Places. First series.

" † Kohl's Sketches in. Kohl was a German, and an accurate observer.

" 1842–'43, Durbin's (Rev. Dr.) Observations in Europe. 2 vols.

Scotland, 1856, Miller's (Hugh) Cruise of the Betsy. Round the North and West.

Ireland, Croker's (T. Crofton) Residence in the South of.
" Thackeray's (W. M.) Irish Sketch Book. Under the name Michael Angelo Titmarsh.
England, 1864, † Hawthorne's Our Old Home.
" Sinclair's (Miss) Scotland and the Scotch.
" 1831, p. Bulwer's (Lord Lytton) England and the English.
France, 1763–'64, * Smollett's (Tobias) Travels through France and Italy.
" 1787–'89, Young's Travels in France. Young was a close observer.
" Pinckney's Travels through the South of France.
" 1803, Holcroft's (T.) Travels in France. Full of information and anecdote. Holcroft was an actor and dramatist.
" 1834, p. Bulwer's (Sir H.) France; Social, Literary, and Political. Bulwer enjoyed good opportunities for this work.
" 1842–'43, Durbin's (Rev. Dr.) Observations in Europe. 2 vols.
" 1851, Head's (Sir F.) A Fagot of French Sticks. Limited to Paris.
Italy, 1701–'03, Addison's (Joseph) Remarks upon Several Parts of. Full upon classical associations.
" 1802–'03, Forsyth's (J. S.) Remarks on Antiquities, Arts, and Letters in. Highly esteemed.
" 1813, * Eustace's Classical Tour through. Has many allusions to classical topics. Not a very good authority.
" 1819, Hoare's (Sir R. C.) A Classical Tour in. A good supplement to Eustace.
" 1837–'38, Tuckerman's Sicily: a Pilgrimage.
" 1850, Flagg's (E.) Venice, the City of the Sea.
" 1853, † Hillard's (G. S.) Six Months in Italy. Admirable.
" 1863, Story's (W. H.) Roba di Roma. A gracefully-written sketch of modern Rome.
" Tyndall's (Prof.) Island of Sardinia.
" Anonymous. * Beaten Tracks: or, Pen and Pencil Sketches in.
" 1867, Chambers's (W.) Something of Italy. Short and sensible.
" 1867, † Howell's (W. D.) Italian Journal.
" 1868, p. Taine's (H.) Italy; Rome and Naples. By a Frenchman, and distinguished art critic.
" " Taine's (H.) Italy; Florence and Venice. This and the last treat chiefly of art topics.
" 1869, Monnier's (Marcus) Wonders of Pompeii.

Switzerland, etc., 1789, Coxe's Travels in.
" 1861, Tyndall's (Prof.) Mountaineering in. Interesting and instructive.
Denmark, etc., 1856–'57, † Taylor's (Bayard) Northern Travel. Includes Sweden, Lapland, Norway, and Denmark.
Norway, 1834–'36, Laing's Residence in.
" 1856, Brace's (C. L.) Norse Folk. Excellent.
Sweden, 1838, Laing's Tour in. Laing's works are in high repute.
" 1854–'64, "By an Old Bushman." Ten Years in Sweden. Full and reliable.
" 1866, Marryatt's (H.) One Year in. Pleasant and instructive.
Russia, 1740, Hannay's (Joseph) Journal of Travel through Russia to Persia; and back through Germany, Holland, etc. Will reward the perusal of the curious.
" 1776–'87, Coxe's Travels in Russia, Poland, Sweden, etc.
" 1842, † Kohl's Russia, St. Petersburg, Moscow, etc. Kohl is always interesting as well as instructive.
" 1847, Custine's (Marquis de) The Empire of the Czar, etc. 3 vols. From the French.
" 1857–'58, † Taylor's (Bayard) Greece and Russia, with a visit to Crete.
" 1862, Edwards's (S.) The Russ at Home, etc.
Hungary, 1716–'17, * Montagu's (Lady) Travels through Germany and Hungary.
" 1851, † Brace's (C. L.) Hungary in 1851. A very pleasing and reliable traveller.
Holland, Anonymous, A Tour in Holland.
Belgium, " Travels in Belgium.
Germany, 1825–'26, Dwight's Travels in the North of.
" Inglis's (H. D.) The Tyrol, with a Glance at Bavaria.
" 1840–'42, Howitt's (W.) Student Life in Germany. From the MSS. of Dr. Cornelius.
" 1840–'42, Howitt's (W.) Rural and Domestic Life in.
" Andersen's (H. C.) Rambles in the Hartz Mountains.
" 1813, p. Staël's (Madame de) Germany. Celebrated. Treats of literature, manners, etc.
" 1851, Brace's (C. L.) Home Life in Germany.
Austria, 1820–'22, Russell's Travels in Germany and Austria.
" 1842, † Kohl's Austria. A storehouse of facts, and yet attractive.

Spain, 1790, * Beckford's Italy; with sketches of Spain and Portugal.
" 1830, * Inglis's (H. D.) Spain in 1830.
" 1836, p. Mackenzie's (A. S.) A Year in Spain.
" 1844, p. Costello's (Miss) Béarn and the Pyrenees.
" 1844, p. † Borrow's (George) The Bible in Spain; also, The Gypsies in Spain.
" 1846, p. † Ford's Gatherings from. The best authority on Spanish travel.
" 1847, Wallis's (S. T.) Glimpses of. Acute and refined.
Greece, 1832–'33, Wordsworth's (Christopher) Classical Tour in Attica, etc. Greece, 1844.
" 1835, † Stephens's (J. L.) Travels in Greece, Turkey, Russia, and Poland.
" 1852–'54, * About's (Edmond) Greece and the Greeks of the Present Day. From the French. Witty and satirical, with lively and withal truthful descriptions.
" 1857–'58, Taylor's (Bayard) Greece and Russsia, with a Visit to Crete. Attractive, as usual.
Europe generally, Travel in.
" 1805–'06, † Silliman's (Prof.) Journal of Travels in England, Holland, and Scotland, etc.
" 1818–'19, Griscom's (Dr.) A Year in Europe. Abounds in valuable information.
" 1834–'38, Laing's Notes of a Traveller.
" 1841, Sedgwick's (Miss) Letters from Abroad.
" 1844–'46, † Taylor's (Bayard) Views Afoot.
" 1847, † Mitchell's (D. G.) Fresh Gleanings.
" 1848–'49, Laing's Observations on Europe in 1848–'49. Forms a second series to Notes of a Traveller.
" 1854, Carlisle's (Lord) Diary in Turkish and Greek Waters.
" 1866, Leech's (H. H.) Sentimental Idler. Travels in Greece, Egypt, and Palestine.
" 1868, Ireland's (Dr. W. W.) Studies of a Wandering Observer.
" " * Freshfield's (D. W.) Travels in the Central Caucasus and Bashan. Novel and instructive.
" " Macgregor's (John) A Thousand Miles in the Rob Roy Canoe. Has written other similar works.
" † Taylor's (Bayard) By-Ways of Europe. Graphic sketches of places little known.

Europe, 1859–'69, Bennet's (Dr. J. H.) Winter and Spring on the Shores of the Mediterranean.

" 1870, p. † Cox's (S. S.) A Search for Winter Sunbeams. Embracing Corsica, Spain, Southern France, North Africa, etc.

ASIA.

Siberia, 1823, Cochrane's Pedestrian Tour through.

" 1828, Erman's Tour in Siberia. 2 vols.

" 1853–'60, Atkinson's Oriental and Western Siberia. Embracing Mongolia, Tartary, etc.

" 1863, † Piotrowski's My Escape from Siberia. Filled with ad ventures that have rarely elicited such daring and perseverance.

Asia Minor, 1838, Ainsworth's (W. F.) Travels in Asia Minor, Mesopotamia, etc. 2 vols.

Armenia, 1830, Parrott's (Dr. F.) Ascent of Mount Ararat.

" 1840, p. Southgate's (H.) Narrative of a Tour in Armenia, Kurdistan, Persia, and Mesopotamia. 2 vols. The curious reader may also consult Curzon's Armenia, etc.

Circassia, 1837, Wilbraham's Travels in Georgia, and Caucasian Russia.

" 1850, p. † Ditson's (G. L.) Circassia : or, a Tour to the Caucasus.

" 1853, Haxthausen's (Baron) Transcaucasia. Speaks favorably of Russian rule.

" 1868, * Freshfield's (D. W.) Travels in the Central Caucasus and Bashan. Corrects errors of Porter.

Babylonia, etc., 1824, Kepple's Travels in Babylonia, Media, Georgia, and Astracan.

" 1845–'47, † Layard's Nineveh. 8vo. An abridged and popular account.

" 1847, Layard's Fresh Discoveries in Nineveh. Both works of great interest.

Syria, 1793–'95, * Volney's Travels through Syria and Egypt.

" 1832–'33, * Lamartine's (de) Travels in the East. From the French. Poetic in style.

" 1835, Addison's Journey from Malta to Greece, Constantinople, Smyrna, Rhodes, Damascus, etc. Written with judgment and taste.—*Kent.*

Syria, 1849, p. * Curzon's (Hon. R.) Visit to the Monasteries of the Levant.

" 1850, Curtis's (Geo. W.) The Howadji in Syria.

Palestine, 1828, * Laborde's Journey to Mount Sinai and Petrea.

" 1838–'56, Robinson's (Rev. Dr.) Biblical Researches in Palestine. A standard authority.

" 1845, p. Warburton's (Eliot) Crescent and the Cross. Delightfully written.

" Thompson's The Land and the Book. 2 vols.

" 1866, Porter's (Rev. J. L.) The Giant Cities of Bashan and Syria. The author has explored a field but little known. Compare with Freshfield's travels.

" Herbert's (Lady) Cradle Lands. Including Egypt, Palestine, etc. See McLeod's * Eastward.

" 1869, p. † Burt's (Rev. Dr.) The Land and its Story. Gives in brief compass a valuable and interesting account of the Holy Land, embodying the latest researches.

Arabia, 1761–'67, Niebuhr's (K.) Travels in Arabia. Truthful and accurate.

" 1835–'36, † Stephens's (J. L.) Incidents of Travel in Egypt, Arabia, Petrea, and the Holy Land.

" 1854, Burton's (R. F.) Personal Narrative of a Pilgrim to El Medina and Mecca. Full of adventure.

" 1862–'63, Palgrave's (W. G.) Narrative of a Year's Journey through Arabia, Central and Eastern. Exciting.

Persia, 1740, Hannay's (Joseph) Journal of Travels through Russia to Persia.

" 1829, Buckingham's (Silk) Travels in Assyria, Media, Persia, etc.

Cabul, 1836–'38, Burnes's (Sir A.) Residence in Cabul.

Central Asia, 1471–'95, Marco Polo's Travels in Tartary. A celebrated Venetian traveller.

" 1829, Humboldt's (Alex. von) Travels and Researches.

" 1831–'33, Burnes's (Sir A.) Travels into Bokhara.

" 1844–'46, Huc's Recollections of a Journey through Tartary, Thibet, and China.

" 1859, Atkinson's (T. W.) Travels in the Region of the Upper and Lower Amoor.

" 1859, Collins's (T. M.) Voyage down the Amoor. By an American traveller.

Central Asia, 1864, Vambéry's (A.) Travels in Central Asia. M. Vambéry—a Hungarian—was sent to Central Asia to investigate its languages. The mission was in the highest degree dangerous, but successfully accomplished. Vambéry gives much information about a region little known, and a narrative full of interest.

" 1868, Vambéry's (A.) Sketch of Central Asia. An appendix to the previous work.

China, Bell's (of Antermony) Travels in China.

" 1836, Davis's (J. F.) China and her Inhabitants. The best work on China, according to Chambers. He has written two other books on China.

" 1842–'47, Forbes's (Lieutenant) Five Years in China.

" 1844–'46, Huc's Chinese Empire. Huc was a French missionary.

" 1847, † Williams's (S. W.) The Middle Kingdom, etc. Abounds in various information.

" 1853, Fortune's Three Years' Wanderings in the North of. Fortune was a botanist of note.

" 1856, p. Meadows's (T. T.) The Chinese and their Rebellion. Full, correct, and philosophical. Has also written "Desultory Notes."

Japan, 1852–'53, Taylor's (Bayard) India, China, and Japan. Pleasant and sensible.

" 1852, Macfarland's Japan.

" 1857–'59. Oliphant's (L.) Earl of Elgin's Mission to China and India, and Japan. Recommended.

Siam, etc., 1857, p. Bowring's (Sir John) Kingdom and People of Siam.

Palmer's (Dr. J. H.) Up and down the Irrawaddy. In the Birman Empire.

" 1863, Mauhot's (H.) Indo-China, Cambodia, Siam, etc. From the French. Throws a flood of light upon a region hitherto but slightly explored. M. Mauhot pronounces the remains of antiquity in Siam, etc., superior to those of India.

India, 1823–'26, Heber's (Bishop) Journal of a Journey through.

" 1831–'33, Burnes's (Sir A.) Travels through Upper India into Bokhara.

" 1832–'34, Earl's (G. W.) Voyages and Adventures in the Indian Archipelago.

India, 1816, Hall's (Capt. Basil) Voyage of Discovery to Corea and the Loo-Choo Islands.

" 1835–'38, Malcom's (Howard) Travels in Southeastern Asia. Embracing India, Malacca, etc.

" 1852–'53, Taylor's (Bayard) India, China, and Japan.

" 1854, p. * "Bohn's" India. Descriptive, pictorial, and historical.

" 1855, Gibson's (W.) My Prison of Weltereden. Exciting.

AFRICA.

Egypt, 1768–'73, Bruce's (James) Travels in Egypt, Nubia, and Abyssinia. An old favorite.

" 1788, † Sparks's (Jared) Life of John Ledyard. Ledyard was a man of genius as well as of a fearless spirit of adventure. His travels embraced Europe, Asia, and portions of Africa.

" 1835–'36, † Stephens's (J. L.) Egypt, Petrea, and Holy Land.

" 1840–'41, Werne's (F.) Expedition to the White Nile.

" 1850, † Curtis's (Geo. W.) Nile Notes of a Howadji.

" 1856, Prime's (W. C.) Boat Life in Egypt and Nubia.

" 1857, * Didier's Fifty Days in the Desert.

" 1860, Pethereck's (J.) Egypt, Soudan, etc.

" 1863, † Speke's (Capt. J. H.) Journal of the Discovery of the Source of the Nile. Captain Speke, it has turned out, was somewhat too sanguine about the extent of his discovery.

" 1865, † Baker's (Sir T. W.) The Albert N'Yanza, Great Basin of the Nile, etc.

" 1867, Baker's (Sir T. W.) The Nile Tributaries.

Hawks's (Rev. F. L.) Monuments of Egypt: or, Egypt a Witness to the Bible.

" 1869, p. Lanoye's (De) Egypt, Three Thousand Three Hundred Years Ago.

Nubia, 1813, * Burckhardt's Travels in. Intrepid, enterprising, and trustworthy. A Swiss by birth.

Abyssinia, 1851–'52, Taylor's (Bayard) Central Africa. From Cairo to the White Nile.

" 1853, Parkins's (M.) Life in Abyssinia. A valuable work in a lively style.

Morocco, 1844, p. Hays's (D.) Morocco and the Moors. See also Lemprière (1790), or Jackson

North Africa,		Gérard's (Jules) Lion Hunting, etc., in Algeria. From the French.
"		Lamping's and De Vance's The French in Algiers. From the German and French.
"	1845, p.	Warburton's (E. L.) Crescent and the Cross.
"		Ditson's Crescent and French Crusaders.
"	1861, p.	Davis's (Dr. N.) Carthage and her Remains.
"		Perry's (Amos) Tunis, Past and Present.
The Sahara,	1845–'46,	* Richardson's Travels in the Sahara.
Central Africa,	1795–'97,	Mungo Park's Travels into. Park revisited Africa in 1805.
"	1850–'55,	Barth's Travels into North and Central Africa. A distinguished German explorer.
"	1855–'59,	† Du Chaillu's (Paul) Explorations and Adventures in Equatorial Africa.
"	1861–'63,	† Burton's (Capt. R. F.) Lake Regions of Central Africa.
"	1864,	Grant's Walk across Africa. "A record of truly courageous endurance."
"	1864–'65,	Du Chaillu's (Paul) Journey to Ashango Land.
Western Africa,	1831,	Allen's Expedition to the Niger. This and the following recommended by Kent.
"	1828–'29,	Morell's (Captain) Third Voyage. Containing excursions into Western Africa.
"		Reade's (W. W.) Savage Africa.
"	1864,	Burton's (Capt. R. F.) Abeokuta and the Cameroon Mountains.
South Africa,	1783–'85,	* Vaillant's Travels in South Africa.
"	1840–'55,	† Livingstone's (D.) Missionary Travels and Researches in. A celebrated narrative.
"	1843–'48,	Cumming's (R. Gordon) Five Years of a Hunter's Life in South Africa.
"	1850–'54,	Anderson's (C. J.) Lake Ngami; or, Explorations in Southwestern Africa.
"	1858–'60,	Anderson's (C. J.) Okavango River.
"	1858–'64,	Livingstones' (D. and C.) Expedition to the Zambesi.
Madagascar,	1853–'54–'56,	Ellis's (Rev. W.) Three Visits to. Our best source of information.

Mauritius, 1857, * Boyle's (C. I.) Far Away: or, Sketches of Scenery and Society in. A pleasant book of travel, and out of the beaten track.

A *Résumé*, 1862, * A General Sketch of Africa. This useful little book shows the ground traversed by the latest travellers.

AMERICA—NORTH, UNITED STATES, MEXICO, CENTRAL.

Canada, 1760–'76, Henry's Travels and Adventures in Canada and the Indian Territories. * Charlevoix's and * Chastelleux's travels (1720) may also be consulted by the curious student.

" 1854, p. Hogan's Canada. Gives full and accurate information.

" 1865, * Milton's (Viscount) Northwest Passage by Land. A trip from Canada through the Hudson Bay Company's possessions to British Columbia.

United States, 1817, Fearon's Narrative of a Journey of Five Thousand Miles in the Eastern and Western States. The inquisitive reader may also consult Carver, 1766; Chastelleux, 1780; and Flint, 1815; but these, like all old books of travel, are rare and expensive.

" 1822, etc., Hall's (Capt. Basil) Travels in North America.

" 1832, † Tocqueville's (A. de) Democracy in America.

" 1836, p. Chevalier's (M.) Society, Manners, and Politics in the United States.

" 1838, Buckingham's (J. S.) Travels in the United States.

" 1839, Murray's (C. A.) Travels in the United States.

" 1841–'42, † Lyell's (Sir Charles) Travels in the United States. A geologist of distinction.

" 1845, Lyell's (Sir Charles) Travels in the United States.

" 1846, Raumer's (F. von) America and the American People. An eminent Prussian historian.

" 1846, Mackay's (A.) Travels in the United States.

" 1851, Johnson's (J. F.) Notes on North America.

" 1853, Chambers's (Robert) What I Saw in America.

" 1854, † Murray's (Capt., the Hon. H.) Lands of the Slave and the Free. Includes, also, Cuba and Canada.

United States,	1857–'58,	Mackay's (Charles) Life and Liberty in America.
"	1859, p.	Kitchi-gami's Travels in Lake Superior.
"	1861,	† Trollope's (A.) North America. Impartial.
"	1869,	Murray's (W. H. H.) Adventures in the Adirondacks. A book for summer tourists.
"	1868, p.	Tuckerman's (H. T.) America and her Commentators. A *résumé* of "Travels" in the United States.
Pacific States,	1836,	Irving's (Washington) Astoria.
"	1838,	Parker's Exploring Tour beyond the Rocky Mountains.
"	1844,	Parkman's, Jr. (F.) California and Oregon Trail.
"	1847–'50,	Colton's (W.) Three Years in California.
"	1849–'50,	† Taylor's (B.) El Dorado. Capital.
"	1852–'55,	Swan's (J. G.) Northwest Coast: or, Three Years in Washington Territory.
"	1854,	Marryat's (F.) Mountains and Molehills.
"	1867–'68,	† Brace's (C. L.) The New West.
The Far West,	1804–'05,	* Lewis and Clark's Expedition up the Missouri and across the Rocky Mountains.
"	1819–'20,	Long's Expedition from Pittsburg to the Rocky Mountains.
"	1837, p.	Irving's (Washington) Captain Bonneville's Adventures in the Far West.
"	1842–'54,	Fremont's Narratives, and Reports to the United States Government.
"	1854,	Oliphant's (L.) Minnesota and the Far West. Readable and instructive.
"	1861,	Remy and Brinckley's Journey to the Great Salt Lake City. A sketch, apparently fair, of Mormon manners and religion. M. Remy was a Frenchman.
"	1862, p.	Burton's (R. F.) The City of the Saints.
"	1864,	Morris's (M.) Rambles in the Rocky Mountains.
"	1865,	Bowles's Across the Continent.
"	1867,	Dixon's (Hepworth) New America.
"	1868,	Browne's (Ross) Adventures in the Apache Country.

The Far West, 1869, p.	Bell's (Dr. W.) New Tracks in North America. Chiefly in Arizona and the Southwest, in 1867–'68.
"	McClure's (A. K.) Three Thousand Miles through the Rocky Mountains.
" 1869, p.	Whymper's Alaska. A work favorably noticed.
Mexico, etc., 1825,	Poinsett's Travels to, and Notes on.
" 1841–'42,	* Mayer's (Brantz) Mexico as it Was, and as it Is.
" 1844, p.	* Kendall's (G. W.) Santa Fé Expedition. See also, if desired, Gilliam's Travels (1845); and Waddy Thompson's Recollections (1846).
Central America, 1839,	† Stephens's (J. L.) Travels in Central America, Chiapa, and Yucatan. 2 vols., 8vo. Excellent.
"	Norman's (B. M.) Ruined Cities of Yucatan. Rich in curious discovery.
" 1857, p.	Squier's States of Central America.
" 1862, p.	" Nicaragua: its People, Scenery, etc.

SOUTH AMERICA AND WEST INDIES.

South America, 1735–'46,	Ulloa's Voyages and Travels.
" 1799–1804,	† Humboldt's (Alex. von) Personal Narrative of Travels in America. [2 vols.
" 1817–'18,	* Brackinridge's Voyage to South America.
" 1820–'22,	Hall's (Captain B.) Journal written on the Coasts of Chili, Peru, and Mexico.
" 1824, p.	Spix and Martius's Travels in Brazil. By two eminent men of science.
" 1826,	Head's (Sir F. B.) Rough Notes of a Journey across the Pampas.
" 1838–'42,	Tschudi's (Dr. J. von) Travels in Peru.
"	* Robertson's (J. and W.) Letters on Paraguay and South America.
" 1849–'52,	Gillis's (Lieutenant) United States Naval Astronomical Expedition to the Southern Hemisphere. 2 vols., 4to.
" 1853–'56,	Page's (Lieutenant) La Plata, the Argentine Confederation, etc.
" 1856–'58,	* Snow's (Capt. W.) Two Years' Cruise off Tierra del Fuego, Falkland Archipelago.
" 1865,	Agassiz's (L.) Travels in Brazil.

South America, 1869, p. Orton's Andes and the Amazon. 8vo.

N. B.—See also, Paez's South America, * Burton's Brazil, and * Hutchinson's Paraguay, etc.

West Indies, 1850, Bigelow's (J.) Jamaica in 1850.
" 1860, Trollope's (A.) The West Indies and Spanish Main. Sketchy, but not without information.

OCEANICA.

Australia, * Leichardt's (Dr. L.) Journal of an Overland Expedition, etc.
" 1831–'35, Mitchell's Expeditions into the Interior of New South Wales.
" 1852, * Sidney's (S.) The Three Colonies of Australia.
New Zealand, Anonymous. New Zealand and its Six Islands.
Pacific, 1843, Jarvis's (J. J.) History of the Hawaiian or Sandwich Islands.
" Cheever's (Rev. H.) Island World of the Pacific.
" Gironnière's (P. de la) Twenty Years in the Philippine Islands.
" 1859, Williams's (Rev. T.) Fiji and the Fijians.
" 1789, * Barrow's (Sir J.) Pitcairn's Island; with an Account of the Mutiny of the Bounty. A story that will never lose its interest. Or see Bligh's account.
" † Wallace's (A. R.) Malay Archipelago.

N. B.—Further information respecting Oceanica can be found, if desired, in the works of Oxley, Westgarth, Martin, the Howitts, Mrs. Meredith, Sturt, Laing, etc.; most of these books are, however, rare.

VOYAGES.

ROUND THE WORLD.

1500, etc., Voyages, etc., of Columbus and his Companions.
1570–1700, Lives, etc., of Drake, Cavendish, and Dampier.
1740–'44, † Anson's Voyages.
1768, etc., † Cook's Three Voyages. In 1768–'72–'76.
1785–'88, † La Perouse's Voyages. From the French
1791–'95, † Vancouver's Voyages.
1818–'41, p. Basil Hall's Fragments of Voyages, etc. Three series.
1831–'36, Darwin's (Ch.) Voyage of a Naturalist.
1834–'36, † Dana's Two Years before the Mast.
1848–'58, Warren's Dust and Foam, etc.

1852–'54, Perry's Exploring Expedition.
Habersham's Exploring Expedition.

Remark.—Some of the above voyages were not, in a literal sense, "round the world." See also * Stanley's Volume of Vasco da Gama, 1497–1553.

ARCTIC AND ANTARCTIC VOYAGES.

1818–'43, Sir James Ross's Voyages.
1818–'45, Sir John Franklin's Voyages.
1819–'25, † Sir Edward Parry's Voyages. Very interesting.
1820–'23, Admiral Wrangell's Expedition, etc.
1839, Sir C. Ross's Antarctic Voyage.
1850, Lieutenant De Haven's Expedition, etc.
1850–'55, † Dr. Kane's Narrative, etc.
1854, † Dr. Hayes's Arctic Boat Journey.
1860–'61, Dr. Hayes's Open Polar Sea.

Remark.—Franklin left home for the last time in 1845. Captain McClintock first brought back (in 1859) authentic intelligence of Franklin's death in 1847. In 1852, after upward of two hundred different expeditions ranging through more than three hundred years, Captain McClure solved the question as to the existence of a northwest passage. McClure went by way of Behring's Strait, having to abandon his vessel (the Investigator) sixty miles west of Barrow's Strait; here he met Captain Belcher, who carried to England McClure and his crew.

COLLECTIONS OF VOYAGES.

Voyages Round the World, from the Death of Captain Cook to the Present Time.
Barrow's (Sir J.) Collections of Voyages up to 1676. 12 vols.

TRAVELS—chiefly by Land—ROUND THE WORLD.

1799–1802, * Clarke's (Dr. E. D.) Travels in Europe, Asia, and Africa. 5 vols.
1841–'42, Simpson's (Sir G.) Overland Journey Round the World. 2 vols.
1853, † Gerstaecker's Narrative of a Journey round the World.
Pfeiffer's (Madame) Travels. Three series.
1858. Minturn's (R.) New York to Delhi.
1868, Dilke's (J. W., M. P.) Greater Britain.
1869, p. Pumpelly's (Prof. R.) Across America and Asia. 8vo.

Remark.—The curious in the literature of travel are referred to St. John's Lives of Celebrated Travellers.

GUIDE-BOOKS—for Intending Travellers.

Appletons' Hand-Book of American Travel. Northern and Eastern Tour. Containing latest information of all lines of travel north of Maryland and east of Ohio, embracing the New England States, New York, New Jersey, Pennsylvania, and the British Dominions; affording descriptive sketches of the cities, towns, rivers, lakes, water-falls, mountains, hunting and fishing grounds, watering-places, sea-side resorts, and all scenes and objects of importance and interest within the district named. 1 vol., 12mo. Flexible cloth. Price, $2.00.

Appletons' Hand-Book of American Travel. Western Tour.

Appletons' Hand-Book of American Travel. Southern Tour.

Easton's Guide to the White Mountains. 12mo, $1.50.

Short-Trip Guide to Europe. 1 vol., $2.00. With Skeleton Tours in America.

Appletons' Illustrated European Guide-Book, with numerous Maps and Illustrations.

Skeleton Tours through England, Scotland, Ireland, Wales, Denmark, Norway, Sweden, Russia, Poland, and Spain. By H. Winthrop Sargeant. 1 vol., limp 12mo.

Saunders's (F.) London, Literary and Historical. A book of the greatest interest and value to the stranger.

* Galignani's Paris Guide. 1 vol., 12mo. * Murray's is, perhaps, equally good. Both are illustrated.

Appletons' New York Illustrated. Profusely illustrated, and desirable as a souvenir of the city.

Moorman's (Dr. J. J.) Mineral Waters of the United States and Canada.

Murray's Hand-Books. Numbering some thirty or forty separate volumes, and published in London. They can be had in this country. They have a high reputation.

Bradshaw's Hand-Books. Several volumes published in London, some adapted for Great Britain, etc., and others for the Continent.

Dr. J. Macpherson's * Baths and Wells of Europe.

Remark.—Plans or maps of the large cities are very useful. The information which they give about localities, public buildings, etc., saves the traveller from that tribe of nuisances, *valets-de-place*, *commissionnaires*, etc. It is better *not* to have the maps bound up with the Guide-Book.

IV.—NATURAL HISTORY.

PHYSIOLOGY, HYGIENE, BOTANY.

THE importance of the study of the natural sciences, as bearing upon intellectual training and practical life, is now pretty generally recognized. This department of knowledge has also other claims upon the student's attention—the modern literature appertaining to natural science is rich in entertainment as well as instruction. Much pains have been taken, accordingly, to collect a choice list of scientific works of a *popular character*, and the perusal of some one or more of these is recommended preparatory to commencing any large text-book.

NATURAL HISTORY.

Agassiz's (L.) Methods of Study in Natural History.
† Agassiz and Gould's Principles of Zoology. First Part. Second part in preparation.
† "Actæa's" First Lesson in Natural History. An admirable little book.
† Wood's (J. C.) Natural History. Homes without Hands. Or, Cassell's, or, Martin's—from the German; or, W. Hooker; or, Maunder's Treasury of Natural History.
Milne-Edward's Manual of Zoology. From the French. Second edition, by C. Blake. This is an excellent compend, forming one of the three which constitute the elementary course of Natural History prescribed by the Council of Public Instruction in France.

Supplemental List.

† White's Natural History of Selborne, Jesse's edition; another charming book.
Agassiz's Structure of Animal Life.
Anonymous, The Journal of a Naturalist.
* † Broderip's Zoological Recreations. Third edition.
* Broderip's Leaves from the Note-Book of a Naturalist. Third edition. This and the last are very popular.

Lyell's (Sir Charles) Geological Evidences of the Antiquity of Man, etc.

† Lewes's (G. H.) Studies in Animal Life. As agreeable in this new field as in philosophy.

Jesse's Gleanings in Natural History. An old favorite.

† Hooker's Child's Book of Nature. One which adults also can enjoy.

* Darwin's (Charles) Voyage of a Naturalist.

Jesse's Anecdotes of Dogs.

* Brougham's (Lord) Dialogue on Instinct. One of "Knight's Weekly Volumes."

Gosse's (P. H.) Evenings at the Microscope.

Brocklesby's View of the Microscopic World.

† Kirby and Spence's Introduction to Entomology. A truly delightful book.

"Acheta Domestica's" Episodes of Insect Life. Three series. Possesses a wonderful charm.

Huber's (F.) Natural History of Bees. A model of patient and careful investigation.

* Samuelson and Hicks's The Earth-Worm and Common House-Fly, in Eight Letters. Well worth reading.

† Figuier's Insect World. From the French. All of Figuier's works have attained unusual popularity.

Figuier's Birds and Reptiles; a Popular Account of their Various Orders, with a Description of the Habits and Economy of the most interesting. By Louis Figuier. Illustrated with 307 Woodcuts.

Figuier's Mammalia: their Various Orders and Habits popularly illustrated by Typical Species. With 267 Engravings on Wood.

Figuier's The Ocean World; a Descriptive History of the Sea and its Inhabitants. With 425 beautiful Illustrations.

De Vere's (Schele) Wonders of the Deep. Full of variety.

Gosse's (P. H.) A Year at the Shore. "Pleasant and chatty."

Hartwig's The Sea and its Living Wonders.

Harper's (John) Glimpses of Ocean Life; or, Rock Pools and the Lessons they teach.

Kingsley's (Charles) Glaucus; or, the Wonders of the Shore. Capital.

* Gosse's Tenby and the Ocean.

Lewes's (G. H.) Sea-Side Studies at Ilfracombe, Tenby, etc. A book which every visitor to the sea-side ought to take with him. The language is plain, and the poetic side of the subject tastefully displayed.—*Westminster Review*, 1858.

Edwards's (A. M.) Life Beneath the Waters; or, the Aquarium in America.

James's (Prof.) The Aquarium Naturalist. Well adapted for popular reading and guidance.

Wood's (Rev. J.) Common Objects of the Sea-Shore; including Hints for an Aquarium.

Agassiz's (B. L. and Elizabeth) Sea-Side Studies in Natural History.

PHYSIOLOGY, MEDICINE, HYGIENE.

† Lewes's (G. H.) Physiology of Common Life. Very instructive, and attractively written.

Bellows's Philosophy of Eating. Entertaining as well as instructive.

† Huxley and Youmans's Elements of Physiology and Hygiene. An admirable introductory work. Or,

Combe's (Dr. Andrew) Principles of Physiology applied to Health and Education. Fifteenth edition in 1860.

Watson's (Dr. Thomas) Practice of Physic. Edited by Dr. Condie. This is a celebrated text-book, able, and written in a most attractive style.

Carpenter's (Dr. W.) Principles of Human Physiology. Of the highest authority.

Agassiz and Gould's Comparative Physiology.

Niemeyer's (Dr. Felix von) Text-Book of Practical Medicine. A late and distinguished German work.

Remark.—With general readers the last three works will answer best for purposes of reference.

Supplemental List.

Flint's Physiology of Man. Designed to represent the existing state of Physiological Science as applied to the Functions of the Human Body. By Austin Flint, Jr., M. D., Professor of Physiology and Microscopy in the Bellevue Hospital Medical College, New York; Fellow of the New York Academy of Medicine; Member of the Medical Society of the County of New York; Resident Member of the Lyceum of Natural History in the City of New York, etc., etc. To be completed in 4 vols:

Vol. 1. Introduction; The Blood; Circulation; Respiration.

Vol. 2. Alimentation; Digestion; Absorption; Lymph and Chyle.

Vol. 3. Secretion; Excretion; Ductless Glands; Nutrition; Animal Heat; Movements; Voice and Speech.

Holland's (Sir H.) Medical Notes and Reflections. From the pen of an eminent physician. It touches upon Electro-Biology, Spiritualism, etc.

Elam's (Dr. C.) A Physician's Problem.

* Physiology of the Senses; or, How and What we See, etc.

Savory's (W.) On Life and Death. Consists of four lectures, and forms a good summary of modern theories of physiology.

* † Smith's (Dr. Southwood) Philosophy of Health, etc. Its popularity has been attested by repeated editions.

Latham's (R. G.) Natural History of the Varieties of Man.

Eyre's (Sir J.) The Stomach and its Difficulties. A useful little volume.

† Brace's (Charles L.) Races of the Old World. Highly esteemed.

Pritchard's Physical History of Man. Upholds the commonly received theory.

Nott and Gliddon's Types of Mankind. Advocates the theory of the diversity of origin of the human race.

Anonymous, Vestiges of Creation, etc.

Darwin's (Charles) Origin of Species by means of Natural Selection. The last two are works of startling interest and great power, whatever may be thought of the views advocated.

Darwin's (Charles) Variation of Plants and Animals in Domestication.

Cabell's (Prof.) Testimony of Modern Science to the Unity of Mankind.

Huxley's (Prof.) Man's Place in Nature.

Huxley's (Prof.) On the Origin of Species.

St. Poole's (Reginald) edition of Genesis of Earth and Man.

Remark.—The "Vestiges of Creation," which, on its first appearance in 1844, created so much sensation, revived the question of the variation of species, originally raised by Lamarck, in 1809. Darwin's "Origin of Species," etc. (published in 1859), infused fresh life into the discussion, which is still actively agitated. The author of the Vestiges calls his theory that of *progressive development.* He and Lamarck mainly agree, and both believe in spontaneous generation. Darwin's may be called the *natural selection*; or *struggle-for-life* theory. Huxley maintains the *gradual modification of preëxisting species.* Agassiz rejects all these theories as unfounded and unscientific. See an article by Asa Gray, in Silliman's Journal for 1862; also, in *North American Review* for 1860.

BOTANY.

† Figuier's Vegetable World. A very attractive book. Well illustrated.

† Gray's How Plants Grow. By a writer of deservedly high reputation.

Gray's Elements of Botany.

Supplemental List.

Coultas's (H.) What may be Learned from a Tree.

Coultas's (H.) Life of a Tree, from the Seed to the Death.

Coultas's (H.) The Plant; an Illustration of the Organic Life of the Animal.

Youmans's (Miss) Botany; elementary.

* Gilpin's Forest Scenery. Last edition. Shows genuine taste.

Macmillan's (Rev. H.) Foot Notes from the Page of Nature. "A very pleasantly written summary of the humblest farms of plant-life."'

Schleiden's Poetry of the Vegetable World. From the German.

† Schleiden's Plant.

Unger's Botanical Letters. Much information in small compass.

Jussieu's (A. de) Elements of Botany. Jussieu has gained high distinction as a botanist.

V.—NATURAL PHILOSOPHY.

ASTRONOMY, CHEMISTRY, GEOLOGY, MINERALOGY.

THE remarks elsewhere made, respecting the practical importance of the study of Natural History and its cognate branches, may be applied with perhaps greater force to Natural Philosophy, Chemistry, etc., etc. It is with these sciences that the human intellect is at present most actively engaged, and it is to the present century that we owe those signal triumphs of man's thought and genius—the locomotive engine, steam navigation, the daguerreotype—making way for the photograph—the electric telegraph, the beautiful and refined speculations as to the laws of light, culminating in the spectrum analysis; not to mention numerous other memorable discoveries, besides great and daring feats of engineering skill.

I have thought it advisable to confine my list of books under the present head chiefly to works of a popular character. The text-books will guide the student to further sources of information, if desired.

NATURAL PHILOSOPHY.

† Silliman's (B., Jr.) First Principles of Philosophy. 8vo. Some knowledge of mathematics required.

Bird's (Golding) Elements of Natural Philosophy. Fifth edition, by C. Brooke.

Lardner's (Diony.) Hand-Book of Natural Philosophy. Edition of 1866, by G. Foster. Lardner possessed unusual skill and clearness in the treatment of scientific subjects. One of the three text-books named would suffice; the similar works by Quackenbos, Comstock, Olmstead, etc., are more elementary.

Supplemental List.

Faraday's Course of Six Lectures on the Various Forces of Matter. The model of a scientific book for the young.

† Herschel's (Sir J.) Preliminary Discourse on the Study of Natural Philosophy. The force and brilliancy of this treatise have been universally admired.

* Arnott's (Dr. N.) Elements of Physics. There is a late edition of this excellent text-book by Dr. Hayes.

Euler's (L.) Letters to a German Prince.

† Brewster's (Sir D.) History of Optics.

Arago's Meteorological Essays. From the French. Arago united the highest scientific attainments with a most attractive style.

† Maury's Physical Geography of the Sea. A deservedly popular work.

Herschel's Physical Geography. From the Enclyclopædia Britannica. "Masterly outlines of well-digested information."

† Guyot's Earth and Man. Scientific, yet attractive.

† Tyndall's (Prof.) On Sound. A course of eight lectures delivered before the Royal Institution. This and the two following works embody the latest information on the subjects treated. They are highly esteemed.

† Tyndall's (Prof.) On Radiation.

† Tyndall's (Prof.) On Heat as a Mode of Motion.

Brewster's (Sir D.) Natural Magic.

Ewbank's Hydraulics. "Of extraordinary research and much curious information."—*Pres. Charles King.*

Youmans's (E. L.) Correlation of Physical Forces. A collection of treatises by Grove, Mayer, Helmholtz, Faraday, Tyndall, etc., giving the most recent theories of dynamics.

Bourne's Catechism of the Steam-Engine. Hand-Book of the Steam-Engine. A key to the "Catechism."

ASTRONOMY

† Herschel's Outlines of Astronomy. 8vo. Of admirable clearness and beauty. May consult Mrs. Somerville's Mechanism of the Heavens.

Arago's Popular Astronomy. Translated by Admiral Smith, etc. Of attractive style.

† Mitchell's (Prof.) Popular Astronomy. An excellent elementary work.

Lockyer's Elements of Astronomy, with charts and illustrations.

Bouvier's (Mrs.) Familiar Astronomy. Highly recommended.

Denison's Astronomy without Mathematics. Any one of these may be selected as a text-book. In cases of difficulty one may throw light upon the other.

Supplemental List.

Lardner's Lectures on Astronomy. As usual, clear and happy in illustration.

Chalmers's (Dr. Thomas) Astronomical Discourses.

Dick's Sidereal Heavens.

Mitchell's Planetary and Stellar Worlds.

Nichol's (Prof.) Contemplations on the Solar System.

Nichol's Architecture of the Heavens.

Nichol's Stellar Universe. Prof. Nichol is easy of comprehension, and pleasing in style.

Hinds's (Prof.) Solar System. Another popular descriptive treatise.

Miller's (Hugh) Sketch-Book of Popular Astronomy. A series of lectures.

Ennis's (Prof. J.) Origin of the Stars, etc. Enters into some interesting speculations respecting the causes of their motions, and their light.

CHEMISTRY.

† Youmans's Class-Book of Chemistry.
Grahame's Chemistry.
Fowne's "
Turner's "
Stöckhardt's "
Hoffmann's "
Roscoe's "
Odling's "

A selection from the text-books will depend pretty much on the student's taste and wants. Special works on single departments are published in profusion. Be sure and get the latest edition. No opportunity of seeing experiments should be lost. It is suggested to commence the study of chemistry with one or more of the books following:

Supplemental List.

† Faraday's Chemistry of a Candle. Very interesting and suggestive.

† Johnston's Chemistry of Common Life. 2 vols., 12mo. Cannot fail to please and instruct.

Liebig's Animal Chemistry.

The food of Man. From "Knight's Weekly Volume."

† Youmans's Household Science.

† Macé's History of a Mouthful of Bread. Servants of the Stomach. The last two from the French.

Griffith's Chemistry of the Four Seasons.

Griffith's Chemistry of the Four Ancient Elements. The last four works are elementary.

* Kemp's (Dr. Lindley) Phases of Matter. 2 vols. An outline of the discoveries of modern chemistry, and of its applications. It is a good summary of the most important facts and doctrines.

Liebig's Agricultural Chemistry.

MINERALOGY, GEOLOGY.

Dana's System of Mineralogy. 8vo. Generally regarded as the best work on the subject.

† Lyell's (Sir Charles) Elements of Geology, etc. 8vo. Edition of 1868, the tenth. Discusses the *ancient* changes of the earth and its inhabitants as illustrated by geology. This is regarded as *the* text-book of the science. In the edition above-named, Lyell, it may be seen, has considerably modified his opinions respecting the theories of Darwin.

Lyell's (Sir Charles) Principles of Geology, etc. 2 vols. Edition of 1863, the ninth. Treats of the *modern* changes of the earth, etc. As a book of reference, Page's Hand-Book of Geological Terms, etc., is recommended. Some one or more of the following works are suggested as preliminary reading.

Supplemental List.

† Agassiz's Geological Sketches. Reprinted from *Atlantic Monthly*. Interesting and instructive.

Page's (D.) Introductory Text-Book of Geology. Edition of 1868, the 7th. Page has also written an advanced Text-Book, fourth edition.

Dana's Geology.

† Miller's (Hugh) Old Red Sandstone.

† Miller's (Hugh) Foot-Prints of the Creator. In reply to the "Vestiges of Creation."

Miller's (Hugh) Testimony of the Rocks. This evoked "The Testimony of the Rocks Confronted," to which Miller replied. Miller's scientific as well as other productions have a wonderful charm and polish of style.

Ansted's The Earth's History.

* Mantell's Medals of Creation. Mantell and Ansted have written extensively and well on geology, but their works are rare in this country.

† Geikie's Story of a Bowlder. Much scientific information most pleasingly communicated.

† Thoughts on a Pebble. Excellent.

† Hitchcock's (Pres.) Religion of Geology and its Kindred Sciences. Highly esteemed.

Smith's (Pye) Geology of Scripture. Edition of 1852, the fifth.

Lyell's (Sir Charles) Geological Evidences of the Antiquity of Man.

MISCELLANEOUS SCIENTIFIC WORKS.

(Embracing Heads IV. and V.)

McDiarmid's Sketches of Nature.

Mudie's Popular Guide to Observation of Nature. Heaven, Earth, Sea and Air. Spring, Summer, Autumn, and Winter.

Bell's Remarkable Phenomena of Nature.

† Hunt's Poetry of Science. Very interesting.

† * Catlin's (Agnes) Drops of Water. A charming little volume.

† "A Traveller's" Frost and Fire; the Natural Engines, etc., with Sketches taken at Home and Abroad. 2 vols. A very instructive and pleasant book.

From * Knight's *Weekly Volume*. The Food of Man.

Kitto's Lost Senses—Deafness and Blindness.

McNish's Philosophy of Sleep. Anatomy of Drunkenness.

Parton's (James) Smoking and Drinking. Condemns both.

Fiske's (Dr. I.) Tobacco and Alcohol. An Antidote. In reply to last.

Miller's (James) Alcohol. This and the next are arguments *against*.

Lizar's (J.) Tobacco. The last two are able prize essays.

Household Words; or, Home and Social Philosophy on Every-Day Topics.

† Youmans's Hand-Book of Social Science. A fund of information upon points of universal interest.

Mayhew's Wonders of Familiar Things. Interesting and instructive.

† Wells's Science of Common Things. A most useful little book.

Peterson's Familiar Science. An improvement on Dr. Brewer's work.

Schœdler's Book of Nature. From the German. A capital elementary book on chemistry, natural philosophy, etc.

Schouw's Earth, Plants, and Minerals; with Kobell's Mineral Kingdom. From the German.

* Knight's (Charles) Scientific World.

* Selection of Scientific Articles from "Dickens's Household Words." May be pronounced unequalled for the skill with which scientific information and entertainment are united.

† Herschell's Familiar Lectures on Scientific Subjects. Edition of 1869.

Somerville's (Mrs.) Connection of the Physical Sciences. Admirable.

Playfair's Discourse on the Progress of Physical and Mathematical Science. The last three authors are particularly eminent.

Brougham's (Lord) Discourses on Science.

Moore's (Dr. G. D.) The First Man, and his Place in Creation.

Harris's (Rev. J.) Pre-Adamite Earth.

† Humboldt's (Alex. von) Aspects of Nature. Picturesque, instructive, and delightful.

† Humboldt's (Alex. von) Cosmos. 5 vols., 12mo. Humboldt combines, to a wonderful degree, clearness of description and a poetic charm of style. His Cosmos is world-renowned.

Whewell's (Prof.) History of the Inductive Sciences.

Whewell's (Prof.) Plurality of Worlds. Defends the negative view.

Brewster's (Sir D.) More Worlds than One. Disputing Whewell's theories.

Anonymous author, Vestiges of the Natural History of Creation.

Huxley's (Prof.) Evidence of Man's Place in Nature.

" On the Origin of Species, etc. Both the last works are held in high estimation.

The "Bridgewater Treatises," eight in number, at present time (1870). They are:

1. Chalmers's (Rev. D.) Adaptation of External Nature to the Moral and Intellectual Condition of Man.
2. Prout's (Dr. W.) Chemistry, Meteorology, and the Functions of Digestion, considered with Reference to Natural Theology.
3. Kirby's (Rev. W.) On the History, Habits, and Instincts of Animals.
4. Buckland's (Rev. Dr.) On Geology and Mineralogy.
5. Bell's (Sir Charles) The Hand; its Mechanism and Vital Endowments, as evincing Design.
6. Kidd's (Dr. J.) The Adaptation of External Nature to the Physical Condition of Man.
7. Whewell's (Rev. W.) Astronomy and General Physics, considered with Reference to Natural Theology.
8. Roget's (Dr. P. R.) Animal and Vegetable Physiology, considered with Reference to Natural Theology.

N. B.—These celebrated works owe their origin to a bequest by the Duke of Bridgewater, by the terms of which the sum of $5,000 was to be paid to the author of the best treatise illustrating the "Power, Wisdom, and Goodness of God." They appear at irregular intervals.

Roscoe's (H. E.) Spectrum Analysis. Comprising six lectures delivered in London in 1868. The subject is one of great interest and scientific value.

* Fullom's (S. J.) Marvels of Science and their Testimony to Holy Writ. Has obtained a wide-spread reputation.

Somerville's (Mrs.) On Molecular and Microscopic Science.

VI.—PHILOSOPHY (Mental and Moral), LOGIC, AND THEOLOGY.

But few works are given on the above heads, as the subjects are not very popular. Metaphysics, included under "Philosophy," is especially a branch of reading—study, it might be said—which few pursue voluntarily; still, as an admirable means of intellectual discipline, and as indispensable to a thoroughly-cultivated mind, it has been thought proper to insert in the catalogue some of the standard works in this branch of knowledge.

In the Appendix will be found additional works on the subject; in all, sufficient to introduce the student to French and the mazes of German philosophy.

PHILOSOPHY—Mental.

Fleming's (Rev. Dr.) Vocabulary of Philosophy, Mental, Moral, and Metaphysical. Edited by C. Krauth, D. D. Useful for reference.

† Lewes's (G. H.) History of Philosophy from Thales to Comte. Or,

Schwegler's (Dr. A.) Hand-Book to the History of Philosophy. From the German. This work is highly commended on all sides.

Morell's History of Philosophy. There is also a good History of Philosophy by Porter.

Cousins's (Victor) History of Modern Philosophy. Clear and brilliant.

Chalybaeus's (Dr. H. M.) Historical Development of Speculative Philosophy. Excellent for readers untrained in speculative studies.

Mackintosh's (Sir James) Discourse on the Progress of Ethical and Political Science. Regarded as a masterpiece among writings of this character.

† Plato's Works. 6 vols. In Harpers' or Bohn's "Classical Library." For most readers a selection from Plato's writings would be sufficient. The most popular are: Phædo, treating of the immortality of the soul and death of Socrates; Protagoras on the Sophists, The Republic, and

Defence of Socrates. Plato is often called the "divine," from the beauty and genius displayed in his works.

Locke's Philosophical Works. With an Appendix by Sir W. Hamilton.

Fichte's Philosophical Works. A most profound and acute thinker, whose works have had deep influence upon philosophy.

Hamilton's (Sir W.) Philosophy. Edition by O. Dwight.

Comte's Positive Philosophy. There is a condensed edition by Miss Martineau, and an excellent book by G. H. Lewes, entitled Comte's Philosophy of the Sciences. Comte is noted for the daring and novelty of his speculations.

Ferrier's Institutes of Metaphysics: the Theory of Knowing and Being. "Since Mill's 'Logic' no English treatise of a metaphysical nature has appeared which will compare with this in interest."—*Westminster Review*, July, 1855.

Hickok's (Rev. L. P.) Empirical Psychology: or, the Human Mind as Given to Consciousness. "The best work on the subject."—*North American Review.*

Supplemental List.

Reid's Inquiry into the Human Mind. Considered the best of his works.

Stewart's (Dugald) Elements of the Philosophy of the Human Mind.

Brown's (Dr. Thomas) Philosophy of the Human Mind, etc.

Alden's (Rev. Dr.) Elements of Intellectual Philosophy.

* Powell's (Rev. Baden) Essays on the Spirit of the Inductive Philosophy.

† Bain's (Alexander) Mental and Moral Science; a Compendium of Psychology and Ethics. 2 vols. A writer "remarkable for the subtleness and clearness of his expositions." The Senses and the Intellect. Pronounced to be his ablest work. Mind and Brain. 2 vols.

Spencer's (H.) First Principles of Philosophy. One of the profoundest thinkers of the day.

PHILOSOPHY—Moral.

Aristotle's Ethics. In Harpers' or Bohn's "Classical Library."

Paley's (W.) Principles of Moral and Political Philosophy. Acute, clear, and most felicitous in illustration, but often unsound in principle.

† Wayland's (F.) Elements of Moral Science. Plain, practical, and trustworthy.

Winslow's (H.) Elements of Moral Philosophy.

LOGIC.

Wilson's (Rev. Dr.) Elementary Treatise on Logic Suited to beginners.

† Whately's (Archbishop) Elements of Logic. Mainly a compilation—well arranged, with a clear and agreeable style.

Tappan's (H. W.) Elements of Logic. Able, comprehensive, and precise.

Mill's (J. S.) System of Logic, etc. The profoundest work on the subject.

THEOLOGY.

Butler's (Bishop) Analogy of Religion, Natural and Revealed, to the Course and Constitution of Nature. A work of undying fame.

Butler's (Bishop) Collection of Sermons. By many considered equal to the Analogy.

Watson's (Bishop) Apology for the Bible. In answer to Paine. He also wrote an Apology for Christianity, in answer to Gibbon.

Paley's (W.) View of the Evidences of Christianity. "The most clear and satisfactory statements of the historical proofs of Christianity in any age or country."—*Robert Hall.*

Paley's (W.) Natural Theology. With notes by Lord Brougham and others. Beautiful in style, but not very profound in reasoning. Paley's Horæ Paulinæ are also much esteemed.

Chalmers's (Thomas) Evidences of Christianity. Written with great force and eloquence.

Rawlinson's (G.) The Historic Truth of the Sacred Records stated anew, etc. "A work of solid and enduring worth."—*North American Review.*

Remark.—The foregoing works, it may be seen, belong chiefly to the evidences of Christianity. On the same subject might be consulted the "Bridgewater Treatises." Under the head "Library," in Appendix, see, if desired, other theological works.

Stowe's (Professor) Origin and History of the Books of the Bible, etc.

Bushnell's (Horace) Nature and the Supernatural, etc.

Hayward's (J.) Book of Religions. Treats of the various creeds, sects, etc., of the world.

† Anonymous, Ecce Homo. See a review by Gladstone in the *New Eclectic* for March, 1868. Much admired, except by the rigid orthodox.

† Baring-Gould's (S.) Origin and Development of Religious Belief.

Supplemental List.

Chalmers's Natural Theology.

† Adams's (Rev. Mr.) Elements of Christian Science.

Taylor's (Thos.) Plato against the Atheists. From the Greek.

Lane's Selections from the Koran.

McCosh's Method of Divine Government. Highly esteemed.

Ecce Deus. Supplements Ecce Homo by upholding Christ's divinity.

Parker's (Theodore) Discourse on Matters pertaining to Religion.

VII.—POLITICAL ECONOMY.

SOCIAL SCIENCE, LAW, POLITICAL SCIENCE.

THE general reader, who may consider political economy, etc., as matters too uninviting to demand his attention, as well as unnecessary, is strongly urged to give some time to each of the subjects treated below. However "dry" they may appear at first, he will find them deeply interesting after some little study. Of their practical importance there can be no second opinion.

POLITICAL ECONOMY.

† Smith's (Adam) Wealth of Nations. Edition by McCulloch. First published in 1776, and still a favorite amid a host of rival works.

† Bastiat's (F.) Essays on Political Economy. Chicago, 1869. The most attractive elementary work on the subject. From the French.

Mill's (J. S.) Political Economy. The sixth edition. There is an abridged "People's Edition." Or,

Wayland's (F.) Political Economy. A sterling work.

Supplemental List.

Bentham's (Jeremy) Letters on Usury.

Ricardo's Political Economy and Taxation. See De Quincey's review of it; Ricardo's Proposition for an Economical and Secure Currency.

Carey's (Matthew) Tracts in favor of a Protective Tariff.

List's Natural System of Political Economy. From the German. Supports a modified restriction.

Knight's (Charles) Knowledge is Power.

Cobden's Political Writings. Edition by W. C. Bryant. Cobden has been called the Apostle of Free Trade.

* Francis's Chronicles and Characters of the Stock Exchange. Very readable.

* Scratchley's Practical Treatise on Savings-Banks, etc. Contains some instructive hints about industrial investments and building societies.

† Knight's (Charles) Capital and Labor; including the Results of Machinery.

Martineau's (Miss) Illustrations of Political Economy. A series of tales, fanciful but forcible.

Wrigley's (Edmund) Workingman's Way to Wealth; a Practical Treatise on Building Associations, etc. Published December, 1869.

SOCIAL SCIENCE.

Buckle's (H. T.) History of Civilization in England. 2 vols. This is a portion of a grand work on civilization which the author did not live to complete.

† Draper's (Dr. J. W.) A History of the Intellectual Development of Europe. Very able and readable, even if the argument is faulty.

† Lecky's History of Rationalism in Europe. Greatly admired.

" " European Morals from Augustus to Charlemagne.

Supplemental List.

† Carey's (Henry) Manual of Social Science. This is a condensation of Carey's larger work by Miss Kate McKean.

Spencer's (H.) Social Status. The work of a profound thinker.

Lytton's (Lord) England and the English.

Bulwer's (Sir Henry) France—Social, Literary and Political. By a brother of Lord Lytton, the novelist.

Balmes's (Rev. J.) Protestantism and Catholicism, compared in their Effects on Civilization in Europe. Represents ably Catholic views of the question.

* Mayhew's (H.) London Poor. Costly.

LAW.

† Kent's (Chancellor) Commentaries on American Law. A standard authority.

† Blackstone's Commentaries, etc. By Judge Shardwood.

† Pomeroy's (J. N.) Introduction to Municipal Law. 8vo. "Comprises much that every educated man ought to know." "Is the only book of the kind."—*North American Review.*

† Woolsey's (Pres.) Manual of International Law. Second edition.

Supplemental List.

Levi's Commercial Law.

Duer's (J.) On Insurance.

Starkie's On Slander.

St. Leonard's (Lord) Handy Book of Property Law.

Wheaton's Elements of International Law. Edition by R. Dana, 1866. Vattell (an old writer) is another recognized authority.

POLITICAL SCIENCE.

† Story's (J.) Commentaries on the Constitution of the United States.

† Curtis's (G. T.) History of the Formation and the Adoption of the Constitution of the United States. 2 vols. The latest and best work on the subject. It contains, besides, notices of the chief framers.

† Hamilton and Madison's, etc. The Federalist. "The best treatise ever written on republican government."—*Kent.*

Sutherland's Congressional Manual. Includes Jefferson's "Manual of Parliamentary Practice." Or,

† Cushing's Manual. Treats of the rules and conducting of public bodies.

† De Tocqueville's Democracy in America. 2 vols. Well worthy of careful perusal. The first volume—the most valuable—has been revised, to suit the changes of the last thirty years, and is published by itself.

Jefferson's (Thomas) Notes on Virginia—about its resources, scenery.

Creasy's (Professor) History of the English Constitution. Brief.

Guizot's Democracy in France.

About's (Edmond) The Roman Question. Witty, but rather satirical.

"A Looker On." The Russian Empire. A view from the American side.

Supplemental List.

Aristotle's Politics.

Dwight's History of the Hartford Convention.

Everett's (Alexander) Tracts on America.

Baldwin's (Joseph) Party Leaders.

Bagehot's History of the English Constitution. Comprehensive.

Hallam's Constitutional History of England. A work of the highest character for ability and impartiality.

† Guizot's History of Representative Government. Excellent.

Mill's (J. S.) Consideration on Representative Government.

† Mill's (J. S.) On Liberty.

Mill's (J. S.) On the Subjection of Woman.

Humboldt's (W.) The Sphere and Duties of Government. By a brother of the philosopher.

† Carlyle's (Thomas) Chartism. Past and Present. Latter Day Pamphlets. The last work treats of "Model Prisons," "Stump Orators," "Parliaments," etc., etc.

† Machiavelli's Prince. This work, by a celebrated Italian of the fifteenth century, has excited much debate. See the opinions of Mackintosh and Macaulay in their collected "Essays."

* Lewis's (Sir J. C.) Essays on the Administrations of England from 1783 to 1830.

Heeren's Politics, Intercourse, and

Trade of the Principal Nations of Antiquity.

Heeren's Reflections on the Politics of Ancient Greece.

Heeren's Political System of Europe.

Everett's (Alexander H.) Europe.

* Brougham's (Lord) Inquiry into the Colonial Policy of the Principal Powers, etc.

* Brougham's (Lord) Political Philosophy.

* Herbert's (Count Münster) Political Sketches of the State of Europe from 1814 to 1868. From the pen of a German publicist.

Louis Napoleon's (the Emperor) Les Idées Napoléoniennes. Translated by J. Dorr.

Louis Blanc's Letters on England.

Sewell's British West Indies.

* Ravenstein's The Russians on the Amoor. An exhaustive monograph of the political history and natural resources of the country.

Remark.—The student in American politics may further consult the works of Morris, Jay, Quincy, Dickinson, John and Samuel Adams, Livingston, etc.

VIII.—DEVOTIONAL WORKS.

THE books named below, it may be observed, do not touch upon sectarian dogmas, nor upon controverted points. The authors belong to the various Christian denominations. The selection of works has been determined by their bearing upon practical piety and their suitability for Sunday reading. A large proportion is biographical, for the influence of example is notorious; besides, in the case of young people, they often read with pleasure an interesting biography, written with taste and judgment, while a formal moral treatise would not tempt them to the perusal of a single page.

BOOKS FOR SUNDAY READING.

† Bunyan's Pilgrim's Progress.

† Taylor's (Jeremy) Holy Living and Holy Dying. Sermons. All admirable.

Barrow's (Isaac) Sermons. Eloquent and profound.

À Kempis's (?) Imitation of Christ. Noted in sacred literature for nearly 450 years.

† Walton's (Izaak) Lives of Donne, Wotton, etc.

† Southey's Life of Wesley.

† Bayne's Christian Life, Social and Individual.

† Farrar's Seekers after God. Includes Seneca, Epictetus, M. Aurelius, etc.

Hare (Archdeacon) and Brother's Guesses at Truth. "Original and suggestive."

† McIlvaine's Evidences of Christianity. Popularly and forcibly written.

† Neander's Life of Christ. Supports evangelical views.

Baxter's Saints' Everlasting Rest.

Hall's (Robert) Life and Works. Edited by Olinthus Gregory.

Foster's (John) Introductory Essay to Doddridge's Rise and Progress, etc.

Doddridge's Rise and Progress of Religion in the Soul.

† Coleridge's (S. T.) Aids to Reflection. "A book to which many owe even their own selves."—*Hare.*

Coleridge's (S. T.) The Friend.

Jay's Autobiography.

Harris's (Rev. Dr.) Mammon.

Wiseman's (Cardinal) Fabiola.

Newman's (J. H.) Callista.

Chateaubriand's Martyrs. The last three are interesting works of fiction, giving pictures of the early Christian Church.

Chateaubriand's Spirit of Christianity. First published in 1802, when it produced most important effects and a great sensation.

Baillie's (Rev. J.) Life of St. Augustine.

Whately's (Archbishop) Historic Doubts about Napoleon. An ingenious *jeu d'esprit* against skepticism.

† Perthes (Caroline) Life of. Daughter of a German publisher.

Abbott's (J.) Corner Stone. Young Christian. Way to do Good. A very sensible and attractive writer.

Taylor's (James) The Natural History of Enthusiasm.

† Neander's Church History. From the German.

Hanna's (Rev. Dr.) Life of Christ.

Vaughan's The Book and the Life. Very popular.

Hanna's (Rev. Dr.) Life and Writings of Thomas Chalmers.

Seymour's Mornings among the Jesuits.

Krummacher's Elijah the Tishbite. David, King of Israel, etc.

Chalmers's (Thomas) Commercial Discourses.

Dick's Christian Philosopher. Has written many other works.

Gosse's Life in its Lower and in its Higher Forms.

Wood's Bible Animals. A pleasant and instructive writer.

James's (Rev. J. A.) Anxious Inquirer.

† Herbert's (George) The Church and other Poems. Quaint and tender.

Coxe's (Bishop) Christian Ballads.

Pollok's Course of Time. Has still many admirers.

† Life of General Havelock. An officer distinguished during the Indian mutiny.

Marsh's (Miss) Life of Captain Vicars. Engaged in the Crimean War.

† Gilley's (Rev. Dr.) Life of Felix Neff. A Swiss Alpine pastor.

Life of Oberlin. A teacher, pastor, and philanthropist, of Strasbourg.

Grimshaw's Memoirs of Rev. Legh Richmond.

Memoirs of George Whitefield and James Ferguson.

Holland's (Dr.) Lessons in Life. Letters to Young People.

† Rogers's (Prof. H.) Eclipse of Faith; or, a Visit to a Religious Skeptic.

Macduff's Mind and Words of Jesus. Morning and Night Watches. Footsteps of St. Paul. Sunset on the Hebrew Mountains, etc.

"Charlotte Elizabeth's" Principalities and Powers in Heavenly Places.

Life of Henry Martyn. A missionary in the East.

Life of Brainerd. A missionary among American Indians.

Hitchcock's (Professor) Relations of Geometry and its Connected Sciences.

" " Religious Lectures on the Peculiar Phenomena of the Four Seasons.

Sparks's (Jared) Collections of Essays and Tracts on Theology from Various Authors, with Notices, etc.

† Keble's Christian Year. It consists of "Thoughts in Verse for the Sundays and Holy Days throughout the Year." Nearly 400,000 copies of this work have been sold within a few years.

Cheever's Lectures on the Pilgrim's Progress.

† Brooke's Life and Writings of the Rev. F. W. Robertson. A man of truly noble character and useful life.

† Robertson's (Rev. F. W.) Sermons.

McCormac's (Dr. H.) Aspirations from the Inner Spiritual Life, etc.

* Newman's (F. W.) The Soul, its Sorrows and its Aspirations. By a brother of the Rev. Dr. J. H. Newman. The first belongs to the rationalistic, the latter to the dogmatic school of Catholicism.

Faber's All for Jesus.

† Guérin's (Eugénie de) Journal and Letters.

Binney's (Sir J.) Fowell Buxton; a Study for Young Men.

Life of Rev. Dr. J. Tauler. Translated by Susanna Winkworth, and edited by Professors Kingsley and Hitchcock.

Smith's Dictionary of the Bible. A very comprehensive work.

Gould's Origin and Development of Religious Belief.

Baillie's Life Studies; or, How to Live. With sketches of Bunyan, Tersteegen, Montgomery, Perthes, etc.

† Peabody's (Rev. E.) Christian Days and Thoughts.

Arnold's (Rev. Thomas) The Christian Life, its Hopes, etc.

† Burt's (Rev. Dr.) The Land and its Story. An interesting account of the Holy Land.

Thomson's (Rev. W. M.) The Land and the Book.

Beecher's Conflict of Ages.

Bateman's Life of Bishop Wilson.

Life of Schwartz.

Zschokke's Meditations on Death and Eternity. On Life and its Religious Duties.

Wayland's Life and Labors of Rev. A. Judson.

† Coleridge's (Sir J. T.) Life of Keble. Author of the "Christian Year."

Evelyn's Life of Mrs. Godolphin.

† Thoughts of the Emperor M. Aurelius Antoninus. Translated by G. Long, for Bohn's "Classical Library." "The purest and noblest book of antiquity."—*Prof. Farrar.*

† Saunders's (F.) Evenings with the Sacred Poets. A truly tasteful pro duction.

† Recreations of a Country Parson. Second and third series.

† Phelps's (Miss E. E.) Gates Ajar. A fiction intended to convey religious lessons.

The Schönberg-Cotta Family Series.

Alexander's Life of J. A. Alexander, D. D.

Conybeare and Howson's Life and Epistles of St. Paul. 2 vols. in one, 8vo.

† Kingsley's (Rev. C.) Village Sermons.

Stories founded on the History of France, Spain, etc. By Society for Promotion of Christian Knowledge.

† Maurice's Religions of the World.

† The Pupils of St. John the Divine. By the author of the "Heir of Redclyffe."

† Maclear's (Rev. G. F.) Apostles of Mediæval Europe.

Falloux's (Count de) Life and Letters of Madame Swetchine. A Russian lady of much social influence in her day, b. 1782, d. 1857.

Miss Luyster's Memoirs and Correspondence of Madame Récamier.

† Duyckinck's (G. L.) Lives of Geo. Herbert, and Bishops Ken, Latimer, and Jeremy Taylor.

† Kingsley's (Rev. C.) The Saints' Tragedy; or, the True Story of Elizabeth of Hungary.

Dick's Works. 5 vols.

† Goulbourn's Thoughts on Personal Religion.

" Introduction to the Study of the Holy Scriptures.

" Office of the Holy Communion, etc.

" Sermons. The Idle Word.

† Macmillan's (publishers) Sunday Library. 4 vols. Comprising:

1. Guizot's Calvin and St. Louis.
2. Macdonald's England's Antiphon.
3. Kingsley's (Rev. C.) The Hermits.
4. Winkworth's (Miss) Christian Singers of Germany.

IX.—POETRY.

To imaginative literature, as embodied in verse, belong the greatest works of human genius in all tongues—great works which never cease their powerful influence upon man's thoughts, emotions, and actions. I take for granted, accordingly, the propriety of devoting a fair portion of our reading to this department. Some give it an almost exclusive attention, reading alike good and worthless poetry; this is a preference quite as regrettable as the distaste which other readers exhibit—a distaste, it may be said, which arises chiefly from pure neglect, and for which the remedy is simple—namely, a little patient, unprejudiced study of a single good poet.

In our hard, practical age, and especially with business and professional men, the claims of poetry and of its sister fine arts are, it seems to me, well worth serious consideration. But, be it observed, it is a taste for the *best* productions only, which should be cultivated; and this remark applies as well with regard to paintings, engravings, music, etc., as to poetry and works of fiction. It is true, our field of enjoyment is thus curtailed, but the enhanced pleasure, the improvement of the nobler faculties, and the time saved from profitless occupation, amply compensate for this drawback. The student is referred to the sections Criticism and Belles-Lettres for guidance and assistance in his poetical studies. I have occasionally appended to the names of the poets some of their best or most popular productions.

AMERICAN POETS—a List of the most eminent.

Halleck, 1795–1868, † Marco Bozzaris. Lines upon the Death of J. R. Drake, etc.

Bryant, 1797– † Thanatopsis. To a Water-fowl, etc.

Longfellow, 1807– † Voices of the Night. Evangeline. The Golden Legend.

Whittier, 1808, † The New Wife and the Old. A Dream of Summer, etc.

Holmes (Oliver Wendell), 1809, † Old Ironsides. My Aunt. On lending an Old Punch-bowl, etc.

Poe, 1811–'49, † The Raven.

Willis (N. P.), 1817–'67, † his sacred poems.

Lowell (J. R.), 1819, † Biglow Papers. Under the Willows, and other poems.

Supplemental List.

Allston.
Aldrich.
Boker.
Brainerd.
Brooks (N. C.)
Coxe (A. C.)
Dana (R. H.)
Davidson (Lucretia and Margaret).
Drake (J. R.), The Culprit Fay.
Emerson (R. W.)
Hoffman.
Holland (Dr. J. G.), Bitter Sweet.
Hopkinson.
Key.
Moore (Miss M. E.)
Morris (G. P.)
Osgood (Mrs.)
Percival (J. G.)
Pinkney.
Prentice.
Sargent (Epes).
Saxe.
Sigourney (Mrs.)
Sprague.
Street.
Taylor (Bayard).
Trumbull (J.), 1750–1831.
McFingal.
Wilde.
Woodworth.

N. B.—See "Selections" and "Collections" of poetry at the end of following list.

ENGLISH, SCOTCH, AND IRISH POETS—a List of the most eminent.

Chaucer, 1328–1400, † The Flower and the Leaf. The Clerke's Tale (from the "Canterbury Tales"). The House of Fame. There are objections to Chaucer on account of his obsolete diction, and on other grounds. The "Chaucer Modernized" obviates many of these objections. A book still better to give a true idea of Chaucer is, I think, a thin duodecimo published by C. Knight, London. This omits a good deal that is uninteresting of the text, and fills up the gaps with brief descriptions in prose, just enough to preserve the continuity of the story. C. Knight has published editions of Spenser, and of some of Lord Bacon's works on the same plan, George L. Craik, editor.

Spenser, 1553–'98, † The Faëry Queen. The first three books are considered the best. See remarks on Chaucer respecting Knight's abbreviated Spenser. Mrs. Kirkland has also edited an excellent family edition of Spenser.

Sidney (Sir Philip), 1554–'86, Sonnets. Arcadia (a small portion of).

Shakespeare, 1564–1616, † Plays. There are numerous editions, varying in number of volumes, and in price. Bowdler's edition is well adapted for family use.

Jonson (Ben), 1574–1637, † Every Man in his Humor. The Alchemist. The Sad Shepherd; an unfinished pastoral. The Fall of Sejanus. Some of his Songs, Masques, and Lyrical Pieces. In these Jonson has shown exquisite grace and beauty.

Beaumont, 1576–1625, Philaster. The Maid's Tragedy. Two Noble Kinsmen.

Fletcher, 1585–1616. Beaumont and Fletcher were associated in the composition of several dramas, but the greater number of the works bearing their joint names were written by Fletcher. The best edition for popular use is Leigh Hunt's, published by Bohn.

Herbert (George), 1593–1634, † Poems. Quaint, but full of beauty and of fervent piety.

Milton 1608–'74, † Paradise Lost. Comus. Lycidas. Il Penseroso. L'Allegro. Sonnets.

Butler (S.), 1612–'80, Hudibras.

Cowley, 1618–'67, Anacreontics.

Dryden, 1631–1700, † Absalom and Achitophel. Ode for St. Cecilia's Day.

Otway, 1651–'85, Venice Preserved (a tragedy).

Addison, 1672–1719, Cato (a tragedy).

Young, 1681–1765, Night Thoughts.

Pope, 1688–1744, † Rape of the Lock. Dunciad. Messiah. Essay on Criticism. Epistles.

Thomson, 1700–'48, Castle of Indolence. Seasons.

Shenstone, 1714–'63, Pastoral Ballads. The School-mistress.

Gray, 1716–'71, Odes and Lyrics.

Collins, 1720–'56, Odes to the Passions; to Evening; on the Superstitions of the Highlanders.

Cowper, 1731–1800, † The Task. John Gilpin. Lines on receiving my Mother's Picture.

Goldsmith, 1732–'74, The Deserted Village. The Traveller.

Sheridan (R. B.). 1751–1816, The Rivals. School for Scandal.

Crabbe, 1754–1832, † The Borough. Portions of the Parish Register.

Burns, 1759–'96, † Poems. Among the best are: The Cottar's Saturday Night. Highland Mary. Tam O'Shanter. The Brig of Ayr. The Mountain Daisy. Ye Banks and Braes. The Twa Dogs. Scots wha hae.

Rogers, 1762–1855, Italy. The Pleasures of Memory.

Baillie (Joanna), 1762–1851, De Montford. Count Basil. Both dramas.

Wordsworth, 1770–1850, † The Excursion. Yarrow Revisited. Sonnets.

Scott (Sir W.), 1771–1832, † Border Minstrelsy. Lay of the Last Minstrel. Marmion. Lady of the Lake.

Hogg, 1772–1835, Legend of Kilmeny (in the Queen's Wake). Hogg wrote under the name of the Ettrick Shepherd.

Coleridge (S. T.), 1772–1834, † Ancient Mariner. Christabel. Genevieve. Translation of Schiller's Wallenstein.

Southey, 1774–1843, Portions of the Curse of Kehama and of Thalaba. Minor poems.

Campbell, 1777–1844, † Pleasures of Hope. Gertrude of Wyoming. Short Poems. Some of the latter are admirable.

Moore, 1779–1852, † Paradise and the Peri (in Lalla Rookh). Melodies.

Hunt (L.), 1784–1859, † Story of Rimini.

Byron, 1788–1824, † Childe Harold. Prisoner of Chillon. Bride of Abydos. The Dream.

Shelley, 1792–1822, † Opening of Queen Mab. Adonais. A Lament for the Death of Keats. Prometheus Unbound. Odes.

Keats, 1796–1820, † Endymion. Hyperion. Eve of St. Agnes.

Coleridge (H.), 1796–1843, Sonnets.

Remark.—Many of the poets in the foregoing list belong to the third or even fourth rank; but I thought it desirable to insert their names, so as to assist the student in recollecting the age when they flourished. Besides, they are, most of them, classic names, around whose memory time has shed a kind of literary halo. The following names are also found in most "Collections of the Poets:" Gay (b. 1688); Mason (b. 1725); Falconer (b. 1730); Churchill (b. 1731); Chatterton (b. 1732); Pollok (1799).

BRITISH POETS AND DRAMATISTS, BORN IN THE NINETEENTH CENTURY, except when otherwise marked.

Aird, The Devil's Dream, etc.

Akenside (b. 1721), Pleasures of the Imagination.

Aytoun, Lays of the Scottish Cavaliers.

Bailey, Festus.

Barnes, Poetry of Rural Life in Common English.

Beattie (b. 1735), The Minstrel.

Browning (Mrs.), † Aurora Leigh, etc.

Browning (Robert), † Dramas. Dramatic Lyrics. Men and Women. The Ring and the Book.

Bulwer (Lord Lytton), Lady of Lyons. Richelieu, etc.

Canning (b. 1785), "*Vers de Société.*"

Colman (the elder, b. 1733), Clandestine Marriage, etc.

Colman (the younger, b. 1762), Comedies.

Cunningham (Allan), Ballads.

Dobell, Keith of Ravelston.

"Eliot (George)," How Lisa loved the King.

Hallam's (Arthur), "Remains in Verse and Prose."

Hemans (Mrs.), Songs of the Affections.

† Hood (b. 1798), Song of the Shirt. Dream of Eugene Aram, etc.

† Horne (R. W.), Orion. A poem of remarkable imagination and power.

† Ingelow (Jean).

† "Ingoldsby Thomas"—(R. H. Barham), The Ingoldsby Legends.

Jerrold (Douglas), Comedies.

Kingsley (Charles), Andromeda.

Knowles (b. 1794), Virginius. William Tell. (Dramas.)

Landon (Miss), some of her minor poems.

† Lytton ("Owen Meredith"), Lucille, etc.

Macaulay (Lord), Lays of Ancient Rome.

† Maginn, Homeric Ballads, etc.

† Massey (Gerald), Ballads.

Milman (Dean), Fazio. Drama.

Mitford (Miss), Rienzi. Drama.

† Moir ("Delta"), short poems.

† Morris (W.), The Earthly Paradise. An exquisite collection of Greek and Romantic legends.

Norton (Hon. Mrs.), some of her short poems.

† Ossian (flourished in the third century), Poems of. The poems Fingal,

Temora, etc., attributed to Ossian, are, probably, chiefly the productions of Macpherson (1760), based on old Celtic ballads.

† Patmore (Coventry), The Angel in the House.

Praed, Poems.

Procter (B. W.)—"Barry Cornwall," his songs.

Procter (Adelaide), her minor poems.

† "Prout (Father)," The Reliques of. The real name of this witty writer was Mahoney.

† Rossetti (Christiana G.), Goblin Market, etc

† Smith (James and Horace), Rejected Addresses. As a series of parodies, unequalled.

† Taylor (H.), Philip van Artevelde.

Talfourd (Sir T. N.), Ion.

† Tennyson (Alfred), Idyls of the King. Regarded as his finest poems. The Princess. In Memoriam. Tithonus, etc.

Remark.—A rather full list of poetical writers has been thus far given. Full as the list is, it might easily have been trebled, and the names of the so-called poets (American and English) would not have been exhausted. Persons not having access to the complete works of the poets, are referred to the selections given below, which will enable them to gather some conception of the different writers, specimens of whom are given.

SELECTIONS OF POETRY—*American and English.*

Griswold's Poets and Poetry of America.

" Female Poets of America. Or,

Bryant's Selections of American Poetry.

Halleck's Selections of English Poetry. Or,

Dana's Household Book of Poetry.

Campbell's (Thomas) Selections of English Poetry. 8vo. Edited by Peter Cunningham. With criticisms.

Griswold's Poets and Poetry of the Nineteenth Century. This supplements Campbell.

Lamb's (Charles) Selections from the Dramatic Poets. Admirably executed.

Hunt's (Leigh) Imagination and Fancy.

" " Wit and Humor

Allingham's Selections of the Choicest English Ballads. About seventy-six in number.

Bell's (Robert) Ancient Poems, Ballads, and Songs, of the Peasantry of England.

King's (R. J.) Selections of Early Ballad Poetry of England and Scotland. Or,
Aytoun and Martin's Bon Gaultier's Book of Ballads. Or,
Hall's (S. C.) Collections of Ballads. Or,
Palgrave's (F. T.) Golden Treasury of the Best Songs and Lyrical Poems in the English Language.
Saxe's Humorous Poetry of the English Language.

COLLECTIONS OF POETS—American and English.

Percy's Reliques of Ancient English Poetry. Gilfillan's edition the best.
Gilfillan's Edition of English Poets. Or,
Child's (Prof.) Edition of the Poets. Or,
Bell's Edition of British Poets. Or,
Wilmott and Duyckinck's English Poets.

FOREIGN POETRY—translated into English.

GREEK POETS.

† Homer's Iliad. There are translations by Chapman, Pope, Cowper, Sotheby, Bryant, Lord Derby, etc. See any of these.
† Æschylus's Tragedies. See Blackie's poetic version, and Mrs. Browning's Prometheus.

LATIN POETS.

Virgil's Æneid; or, his Eclogues.
Terence's Comedies, a portion of.
Horace's Odes. Translations of the poets named can be seen in Harper's "Classical Library," and elsewhere. Or,
† Elton's Specimens of the Greek and Latin Poets. 3 vols.

GERMAN POETS.

† Goethe's Faust. Translated by Hayward, Brooks, etc. Iphigenia; Goetz von Berlichingen. Translated by Sir W. Scott. Lyrics. Translated by Aytoun and Martin.
† Schiller's William Tell. Wallenstein. Admirably translated by Coleridge. Lyrics. Translated by Bulwer and others.
Wieland's Oberon. Translated by Sotheby.
Lessing's Nathan the Wise. Translated by Miss Frothingham.
† Heine's Book of Songs. Translated by Leland. His complete poems, by E. A. Bowring.

Bürger's Leonora, Wild Huntsman, and Ballads. Translated by Sir W. Scott, etc.

Körner's Lyre and Sword Songs.

Uhland's Poems. Translated in part by Longfellow, etc. See also Baskerville's † "Specimens of German Poetry" (translated); and C. T. Brooks's "Songs and Ballads translated from Uhland," etc., etc.

ITALIAN POETS.

† Dante's Comedy. Usually called the Divine Comedy—Divina Commedia. Translated by Cary and by Longfellow.

Tasso's Jerusalem Delivered. Translated by Fairfax, Hoole, Wiffen, and others.

MISCELLANEOUS POETRY.

Foreign.

† Spanish—See Lockhart's "Spanish Ballads."

French—Béranger's Lyrical Poems. Translated by W. Young.

" La Fontaine's Fables. Translated by E. Wright.

Danish—Hertz's King René's Daughter. Lyric drama.

Various—Longfellow's † "Poets and Poetry of Europe."

" Bowring's "Specimens" of same.

" Alger's "Poetry of the East."

X.—BELLES-LETTRES.

PHILOLOGY, CRITICISM, FINE ARTS.

Some departments popularly belonging to Belles-Lettres, for instance, history and poetry, have been placed elsewhere. For convenience' sake, no rigidly-correct division of the subjects has been followed. Under the head "Essays," will be found much matter relating to criticism proper.

The scope of the work precludes any mention of illustrated works, collections of engravings, etc. For the same reason no attempt has been made to present lists of musical compositions

BELLES-LETTRES.

Duyckinck's (E. A. and G.) Cyclopædia of American Literature. 2 vols., 8vo. With supplement, bringing it down to 1865.

† Shaw's (T. B.) Manual of English Literature. 1 vol., 12mo. Has a sketch of American literature by Tuckerman.

Craik's (George L.) Compendious History of the English Language and of English Literature, etc. 2 vols., 8vo.

Chambers's Cyclopædia of English Literature. 2 vols., 8vo.

Browne's (R. W.) Histories of Greek and Roman Literature. 2 vols.

† Foster's (Mrs.) Hand-Book of Modern European Literature.

† Disraeli's (Isaac) Curiosities of Literature.

Magoon's (Dr.) Orators of the Revolution.

Supplemental List.

Disraeli's Quarrels of Authors. Calamities of Authors. Amenities of Literature.

† Wilson's (Prof. J.—the "Christopher North" of Blackwood's Magazine) Recreations of Christopher North. 2 vols. Noctes Ambrosianæ. 4 vols. A series of dialogues, abounding in genial wit.

Hazlitt's Conversations with J. Northcote.

Grimm's (Baron de) Historical and Literary Anecdotes. From the French.

Cunningham's (A.) Biographical and Critical History of the Last Fifty Years. Died in 1842.

Burke's (Edmund) On the Sublime and Beautiful.

Alison's (Rev. Archibald) Essay on Taste.

American Eloquence.

Goodrich's Specimens of British Oratory.

† Schlegel's Æsthetic and Miscellaneous Works. 1 vol. Bohn's edition.

† White's (R. G.) Shakespeare's Scholar.

Campbell's (Lord) Shakespeare's Legal Acquirements considered.

Stearns's (Dr. C. W.) Medical Knowledge of Shakespeare.

Bucknell's (Dr. J. C.) Medical Knowledge of Shakespeare. For criticisms on Shakespeare's poetical works, see section "Criticism" under the present head.

† Felton's, Sears's, etc., Ancient Literature and Art.

Felton's (Prof.) Ancient and Modern Greece. 2 vols.

Schlegel's History of Literature, Ancient and Modern.

Hallam's Introduction to the Literature of Europe in the Fifteenth, Sixteenth, and Seventeenth Centuries.

Sismondi's Historical View of the Literature of the South of Europe.

* Véricour's Course of French Literature.

Chambers's Italian Literature.

Menzel's History of German Literature.

Hedge's Prose Writers of Germany, with extracts from their works.

Chambers's German Literature. Judicious and compendious.

Solling's (Gustav) Review of the Literary History of Germany to the Nineteenth Century.

Howitt's (W. and M.) Literature and Romance of Northern Europe.

Talvi's Slavic Language and Literature.

Ticknor's History of Spanish Literature. 3 vols.

Max Müller's History of Ancient and Sanscrit Literature.

Max Müller's Comparative Mythology.

† Cox's (Rev. G. W.) Manual of Mythology. Mythology of the Aryan Nations. Tales of the Gods and Heroes. Tales of Thebes and Argos, etc.

PHILOLOGY.

† Latham's English Grammar. Or, Fowler's Hand-Book of the English Language.

† Alford's (Dean) Plea for the Queen's English. Sensible, and very pleasantly written.

† Moon's Defence of the Queen's English. The Dean's English. Bad English.

† Trench's (Archbishop) Study of Words. Lectures on English, Past and Present. [See below.]

† Marsh's (Geo. P.) Lectures on the English Language. Origin and History of the English Language.

† Whitney's (Prof.) Language, and the Study of Language.

Dwight's Modern Philology.

Müller's (Max) Lectures on Language. Science of Language. Two series.

Supplemental List.

† De Vere's (Prof. Schele) Studies in English.

Trench's (Archbishop) New Lectures on English, Past and Present. Archbishop Trench, lately archdeacon, is a very popular as well as voluminous writer. Not to touch upon his religious works, he has also written, in the department of philology, "Some Deficiencies in our English Dictionaries."

Johnson's Meaning of Words.

Swinton's (W.) Rambles among Words.

Tooke's Diversions of Purley. The oldest book in our list, published 1786, also ingenious and original, but often erroneous.

Payne's (J.) Studies in English Prose. A capital book for the young student.

Farrar's (Rev. F.) Origin of Language. Chapters on Language. Families of Speech.

Key's (T. Hewitt) Philological Essays.

† Haldeman's (Prof. S. S.) Affixes to English Words. An admirable book of reference in etymology.

Wedgewood's Dictionary of English Synonymes. Edited by G. P. Marsh.

CRITICISM—Literary.

† Reed's (Prof. H.) Lectures on English Literature. Lectures on the British Poets. 2 vols., 12mo. Lectures on English History and Tragic Poets. All these works are marked by singular beauty of style, and refined critical taste.

Taine's (H.) English Literature. "The most elaborate and valuable that now exists."—*Westminster Review*, 1864.

† Coleridge's (S. T.) Lectures on Shakespeare, and other Dramatists. Coleridge, from the peculiar bent of his mind, his scholarship, and, above all, from his true poetic genius, was admirably suited to the office of critic.

† Thackeray's (W. M.) English Humorists.

Masson's British Novelists and their Styles.

Supplemental List.

Campbell's (Thomas) Essay on English Poetry, with Notices of British Poets.

Holmes's (O. W.) English Poets of the Nineteenth Century.

Lowell's (J. R.) Conversations on Some of the Old Poets. Among My books.

Addison's (Joseph) Criticism on Milton.

† Hazlitt's Lectures on the English Poets. Lectures on the Literature of the Elizabethan Age. Dramatic Essays. View of the English Stage. Lectures on the English Stage.

Dryden's (John, the poet) Essay on Dramatic Poetry.

Schlegel's (A. W.) Lectures on Dramatic Criticism.

Girardin's Lectures on Dramatic Literature.

Knight's (C.) Studies of Shakespeare.

† Jameson's (Mrs.) Female Characters of Shakespeare.

* Clarke's (C. Cowden) Shakespeare's Characters.

Guizot's Shakespeare and his Times.

Ulrici's Shakespeare's Dramatic Art, and its Relation to Calderon and Goethe.

Greene's Shakespeare and the Emblem Writers of his Age.

Kames's (Lord) Elements of Criticism.

* Drake's Literary Hours.

Poe's (Edgar A.) Critical Papers in his Miscellaneous Writings.

Chasles's (Philarète) Anglo-American Literature and Manners. From the French.

Wallace's (H. Binney) Literary, Critical, and other Papers.

Jeaffreson's Novels and Novelists. 2 vols. Down to 1858.

Fuller's (Margaret) Papers on Literature and Art.

FINE ARTS.

Reynolds's (Sir Joshua) Discourses on the Theory and Practice of Painting.

† Samson's (G. W.) Elements of Art Criticism. There is an abridgment.

Haydon and Hazlitt's On Painting and the Fine Arts.

† * Ruskin's Modern Painters. 5 vols. Aims to prove the superiority of modern landscape painters, especially Turner, over their ancient predecessors. Seven Lamps of Architecture. 1 vol. Stones of Venice. 3 vols. (Subject, architecture.) Queen of the Air. 1 vol., 12mo, 1870, etc. Ruskin's writings produced an art revolution in Great Britain. He is a warm supporter of pre-Raphaelism. Mrs. Tuthill has edited a selection from his works, entitled "The True and the Beautiful." 1 vol., 12mo.

† Jarvis's (J. J.) Art Idea, Sculpture, Painting, and Architecture in America. Excellent.

† Tuckerman's (H. T.) Book of the Artists.

Supplemental List.

† Haydon's Autobiography. Of mournful interest.

Spooner's Anecdotes of Painters, Engravers, Sculptors, and Architects. 3 vols. Lives of Wilkie, Lawrence, and Fuseli.

Cunningham's (Allan) Lives of the British Sculptors. See, if desired, in Vasari the lives of the most eminent painters of mediæval times.

Benvenuto Cellini's Autobiography. Under the head "Biography" may be found other lives of artists.

Howitt's (Miss) Art Student in Munich.

Jameson's (Mrs.) Early Italian Painters. Sacred and Legendary Art. Legends of the Madonna. Sketches of Art.

Fuller's (Margaret) Essays on Literature and Art.

Eastlake's (Sir C. L.) Contributions to the Literature of the Fine Arts.

Potter's (Bishop) Sculpture and the Arts.

Burney's (Dr.) History of Music.

Fuseli's Lectures on the Fine Arts. See also his Life by Knowles.

Hazlitt's Criticism on Art.

Taine's Philosophy of Art. The Ideal in Art. Italy.

Allston's (W.) Lectures on the Fine Arts. Much admired.

Palgrave's (F. T.) Essays on Art. Contains also sensible remarks on literature, the drama, etc.

Arnold's (Matthew) Art Criticism. Deservedly esteemed.

Lamb's (Charles, "Elia") Essay on the Genius of Hogarth. Deemed by many the finest piece of art criticism in English. To be found in Lamb's collected works.

Goethe's Essays on Art.

Lessing's Essay on the Laocoon. A splendid piece of criticism.

Winckelman's History of Ancient Art among the Greeks. All three old writers, but most eminent. Winckelman, in his field, was unequalled.

XI.—ESSAYS.

MISCELLANIES, TABLE-TALK, ANA, LECTURES, ETC.—DIDACTIC IN CHARACTER.

THE modern essay, so much more comprehensive in its scope, and generally so much profounder in its nature, than in the days of Addison, occupies at present quite an important position in literature. As a rule, it forms delightful reading, able and scholarly, and upon all kinds of subjects: there are, accordingly, but few readers who will not find something to please them in our numerous modern collections. These are chiefly made up of articles from reviews, magazines, etc., and reprinted in book-form.

ESSAYS, Etc.

ENGLISH, AMERICAN, FOREIGN.

† Bacon's (Lord) Essays. Edition by Whately, or, still better, the edition by Little, Brown & Co. For three centuries have delighted all readers.

Addison and Steele's Essays, as selected by Mrs. Barbauld from the *Spectator*. 2 vols. Or by † Tegg.

† Foster's (John) Essays on Decision of Character. On Improvement of Time. On the Evils of Popular Ignorance. Of uncommon power and worth. [See also below.]

† De Quincey's Essays, biographical, historical, critical, etc. Also of rare worth and beauty.

Hazlitt's Winterslow Essays. So called from the place where written. [See below.]

† Lamb's (Charles) Essays by "Elia." For graceful wit and humor, hardly equalled.

† Macaulay's Essays. Very attractive from their brilliant, picturesque style.

Carlyle's (Thomas) Essays Display deep and original thought. The style, unfortunately, is very affected.

† Helps's (Arthur) Friends in Council. Two series. [See below.]

† Emerson's Essays. Representative Men. English Traits. Lectures. Another profound and original thinker.

Whipple's Characters. Characteristic Men. Highly esteemed.

† Tuckerman's Criterion and Optimist Essays. Short essays on familiar subjects, delightfully written, and in refined taste.

† Montaigne's Essays. Have amused and instructed readers for upward of three centuries.

Supplemental List of English Essays, etc.

Cowley's Essays. The Tatler (established in 1709). The Spectator (1711). The Rambler. The contributions of Addison to the Tatler and Spectator, and of Dr. Johnson to the Rambler, give their chief value to these magazines.

Shenstone's Essays. The Mirror and Lounger. Scotch periodicals, mainly consisting of articles by MacKenzie; of value mostly as literary curiosities.

Mackintosh's Essays.

Smith's (Sydney.) Noted for their wit and good common-sense.

Wilson's (Prof.) Essays, critical and imaginative.

Jeffrey's Essays.

Coleridge's Essays on His Own Times, chiefly English politics.

Southey's Essays.

Hallam's.

Hunt's (Leigh) Indicator and Companion.

Hazlitt's Round-Table. Political Essays: with Sketches of Public Characters. A charming writer; also, an able and acute critic.

Broughman's (Lord) Contributions to the Edinburgh Review.

Mill's (J. S.) Dissertations and Discussions. The best adapted of all his writings to popular reading.

Buckle's Essays.

Alison's (Sir James) Essays.

Stephen's (Sir James).

Miller's (Hugh). Edited by Peter Bayne.

Hamilton's (Sir W.) Discourses on Philosophy and Literature, etc.

Helps's (Arthur) Essays. Written in the intervals of business. A writer sure to please and to instruct, while at the same time his counsel never wearies us.

Spencer's (Herbert) Essays, etc. One of the profoundest thinkers of the day.

Arnold's (Matthew) Essays.

Müller's (Max) Chips from a German Workshop. 3 vols. By the celebrated philologist.

Brown's (Dr. J.) Spare Hours. Two Series.

† "A Country Parson's" Recreations. 2 vols.

Leisure Hours. By Rev. A. H. Boyd, of Scotland. [See also other works of this admired writer, under the head "Devotional."]

Talfourd's Essays.

† Bayne's (Peter).

Kingsley's (Rev. Charles).

Senior's.

Chambers's Selected Writings. 5 vols. "Afternoon Lectures" on Literature and Art. Delivered by various speakers in Dublin.

Remark.—The order in which the essayists have been named is, in the main, chronological, not in the order of merit.

Supplemental List of American Essays, etc.

† Channing's Essays and Discourses. A writer of exquisite purity and polish.

Story (Joseph), Selections from the Writings of.

Wheaton (R.), Selections from the Writings of.

Everett's (Edward) Essays.

Everett's (Alex. H.) The last four, men of public and literary fame.

Prescott's Miscellanies. From the polished pen of the historian.

Fuller's (Margaret) (Marchioness d'Ossoli) Life Within and Life Without. A Series of Reviews, Essays, etc.; perhaps her most popular writings.

Bancroft's Miscellanies.

Holland's (Dr.) ("Timothy Titcomb") Gold Foil. Essays on all kinds of subjects. With a moral tendency.

Hawthorne (Nathaniel), Passages from the American Note-Books of. Also from the English and Italian Note-Books.

Giles's (H.) Illustrations of Genius.

Bigelow's (Dr. J.) Modern Inquiries.

Supplemental List of Foreign Essays, etc.

† Grimm's (H.) Essays. Criticisms on Shakespeare, Dryden, Byron, Macaulay, etc.

Renan's (Ernest) Essays on Religious History.

Essays, Moral and Critical.

† Sainte-Beuve's Portraits of Celebrated Women. His Causeries du Lundi, a publication, in book-form, of contributions to La Revue de Paris, and Le Constitutionnel, have a brilliant reputation, but, I think, have not appeared in English. They were elaborated with great care, and extend through several volumes.

La Bruyère's Characters. Owed much of its fame to allusions to persons living at the time of publication (1687).

TABLE-TALK, ANA, Etc.

Selden's Table-Talk. Flourished 1584–1654.

Southey's (Dr.) Commonplace Book. Omniana.

Landor's Imaginary Conversations of Literary Men and Statesmen. 5 vols.

Supplemental List.

† Luther's Table-Talk. Edited by Hazlitt, or Carlyle.

Pascal's (1623–'62) Thoughts.

Rochefoucauld's Maxims.

Bonaparte's (Napoleon) Table-Talk. Opinions. Maxims.

Wellington's Maxims.

Hazlitt's Table-Talk.

Hunt's (Leigh) Table-Talk. Imaginary Conversations between Pope and Swift.

Rogers's Table-Talk, with Porsoniana. The termination *ana* is frequently added to names to designate collections of anecdotes, sayings, etc.

Fosteriana. Thoughts, Reflections, and Criticisms of John Foster.

Benthamiana. Chiefly selections from Bentham's writings.

† Coleridge's Omniana, Table-Talk, Bulweriana, etc., etc.

XII.—MEMOIRS, LETTERS.

RECOLLECTIONS, JOURNALS, AUTOBIOGRAPHIES, Etc.

MEMOIRS—American.

† Lee's (Henry) Memoirs of the Southern Campaign (1781). New edition by Gen. R. E. Lee. A very graphic and trustworthy narrative.

Watson's (Elkanah) Men and Times of the Revolution. Interesting and instructive.

Rush's (R.) Memoranda of a Residence at the Court of St. James in 1817–'19. Memoranda of a Residence at the Court of London, from 1819 to 1825. Occasional Productions; Political, Diplomatic, and Miscellaneous.

Schoolcraft's Personal Memoirs of a Thirty Years' Residence with the Indian Tribes on the American Frontier, etc.

Nolte's (Vincent) Fifty Years' Residence in Both Hemispheres. 1779–1829.

Gobright's Men and Things at Washington during the Third of a Century. To present times.

MEMOIRS—English.

* Aikin's (Miss Lucy) Memoirs of Charles I. Commended by Prof. Smyth.

† Hutchinson's (Mrs.) Memoirs. An interesting and unprejudiced account of the men and the times in the Civil War, 1642–'49. Mrs. Hutchinson wrote also Life of Col. J. Hutchinson, which is highly esteemed.

* Herbert of Cherbury's (Lord) Memoirs. The record of a truly adventurous life, d. 1648.

Thomson's (Mrs.) Memoirs of the Duchess of Marlborough and the Court of Queen Anne.

Colley Cibber's Apology. 1671–1757. "Apology" is here used in its old sense of defence, vindication.

Walpole's (Horace) Memoirs of the Last Ten Years of the Reign of George II.

Wraxhall's Memoirs of his Own Times. 1751–1831. Excellent.

† Grant's (Mrs.) Memoirs of an American Lady. 1735–'38. Contains a rich fund of anecdote.

Cumberland's (R.) Memoirs. 1732–1811. Edited by H. Flanders. Cumberland, as a dramatist, diplomatist, and a man who mixed in the best society, literary and political, had naturally much of interest to relate.

Somerville's (Thomas) My Own Life and Times. 1741–1814. Somerville was a minister at Jedburg, Scotland. He gives a picture "racy and hearty" of the persons and manners of his day.

Barrington's (Sir Jonah) Historical Memoirs of Ireland, comprising Secret Records of the National Convention, of the Rebellion of '98, and of the Union. 2 vols.

Cockburn's (Henry) Memoirs of His Times. Became a Scotch judge, and was intimate with Sydney Smith, Brougham, Jeffrey, etc.

* Madden's (R.) The United Irishmen; their Lives and Times.

Gordon's (Mrs.) Memoirs of Prof. Wilson, the genial, manly "Christopher North." Mrs. Gordon was his daughter.

MacIlwain's Memoirs of Abernethy.

MEMOIRS—Foreign.

Comines's (Philippe de) Memoirs. 1445–1509. To these memoirs we owe most of our knowledge of the character and policy of Louis XI. of France.

* De Retz's (Cardinal) Memoirs. 1614–'79.

* Saint Simon's (Duc de) Memoirs. 1675–1755. Valuable information and striking portraits of character, but mixed with much gossip and scandal. There is a condensed translation by B. St. John in 3 vols. Original edition (French) in 13 vols.

Campan's (Madame) Memoirs. By a faithful friend of the unfortunate Marie Antoinette.

† La Rochejacquelein's (Marquis) Memoirs. A thrilling narrative of adventures and sufferings in the revolutionary times of France.

Roland's (Madame) Memoirs. Of great interest.

† Bonaparte's (Napoleon) Memoirs. Dictated at St. Helena.

Marmont's (Marshal) Memoirs.

Junot's (Marshal) Memoirs. The three works last named are important to the student of the French Revolution.

Talleyrand's (Prince of Benevento) Memoirs. The publication of these was deferred by will until 1868. I am not sure whether a translation has been made into English.

Villemain's Memoirs. Valuable from the notices which he gives of his contemporaries.

Véron's Memoirs of a Bourgeois of Paris. Full of musical, dramatic, and literary gossip, anecdotes, etc.

Miot's (Count de Meleto) Memoirs. A very lively and generally trustworthy account of French affairs from 1815 to 1830.

Houdin's Memoirs. A celebrated French conjurer. Very amusing.

† Pellico's (Silvio) My Prisons. A pathetic story. Pellico was an Italian poet and political martyr.

RECOLLECTIONS AND REMINISCENCES—American and English.

Farrar's (Mrs. John) Recollections of Seventy-one Years.

* Thorburn's (Grant) Fifty Years' Reminiscences of New York. 1792–1842. Wrote under the name Laurie Todd.

Francis's (Dr. J. W.) Reminiscences of the Last Sixty Years. 1793–1857. Or, Old New York.

Parker's (E. C.) Reminiscences of Rufus Choate.

* Goodrich's (S. G.) Recollections of a Lifetime.

Greeley's (Horace) Recollections of a Busy Life.

Kelly's Reminiscences of the Stage.

† Ramsey's (Dean) Recollections of Scottish Life and Character. "A classic collection of stories of Scottish wit and humor."

* Dibdin's Reminiscences of a Literary Life. Dibdin was noted for his bibliographical tastes.

Mitford's (Miss) Recollections of a Literary Life.

McLeod's (Norman) Reminiscences of a Highland Parish. Very entertaining.

JOURNALS AND DIARIES.

† Pepys's Diary. 1620–'93. Edited by Lord Braybrooke. Full of a *naïve* gossip which gives a livelier picture of the persons and manners of his day than any history.

Evelyn's Diary. 1620–1705. Edition of 1854 the best. Sir Walter Scott said "he had never seen a mine so rich."

† "Willoughby's" (Lady) Diary. Of the times during the Civil War in Charles I.'s reign. It is fictitious, but with an air of reality truly ingenious.

† Adams's (John) Diary and Letters. A valuable help to the knowledge of American history.

† Curwin's (Samuel) Journal and Letters. Fourth edition, edited by G. A. Ward. Another most valuable and deservedly popular contribution to American history.

D'Arblay's (Madame) Diary. 1752–1840. By Fanny Burney, the author of Evelina, etc.

Berry (Miss), Extracts from the Journal and Correspondence of. 1783–1852. Edited by Lady Lewis. Rather diffuse, but much information may be gleaned, which could not readily be found elsewhere.

Guérin's (Maurice de) Journal; with an Essay by Matthew Arnold, and a Memoir by Sainte-Beuve. From the French by E. T. Fisher.

Victoria's (Queen) Leaves from the Journal of our Life in the Highlands.

† Robinson's (Henry Crabb) Diary. A fund of varied anecdote, extending over three-fourths of a century. Published 1869.

AUTOBIOGRAPHIES.

† Franklin's (Benjamin) Autobiography. There are several editions, including a recent one by J. Bigelow.

Jefferson's (Thomas) Autobiography.

Mowatt's (Mrs.) Autobiography of an Actress. A very interesting book.

Hume's (David) Autobiography. 1711–'76. By the historian and philosopher.

Gibbon's Autobiography. The Historian. 1737–'94.

Piozzi's (Madame) Autobiography; Letters and Literary Remains. 1739–1821. Better known under the name of Mrs. Thrale, and a warm friend of Dr. Johnson. Edited by Edward A. Hayward.

* Gifford's Autobiography. The poet and critic. 1756–1826.

* Barrow's (Sir J.) Autobiography. Naval Officer, etc. 1764–1848

† Borrow's (George) Autobiography. Author of the Gypsies in Spain, etc.

Crockett's (D.) Autobiography.

Haydon's Autobiography. The painter. 1786–1846.

Hunt's (Leigh) Autobiography. 1784–1864.

† De Quincey's Confessions of an Opium-Eater. Autobiographic Sketches of great beauty and force.

Leslie's Autobiography. The painter.

Carlyle's (Dr.) Autobiography. One of the most interesting works on medical biography.

† Cellini's (Benvenuto) Autobiography. A Florentine sculptor and engraver. 1500–'70. A work of extraordinary interest.

Alfieri's Autobiography. A Piedmontese dramatist. 1749–1803.

Goldoni's Autobiography. A Venetian dramatic writer, theatrical manager, etc. 1707–'93. Very entertaining.

Stilling's Autobiography. A German professor, etc. 1740–1817. A most singular book.

Goethe's Autobiography. Edited by Parke Godwin.

Vidocq's Autobiography. A celebrated French detective.

Steffin's Story of my Career, etc. A professor at Halle.

Béranger's Autobiography. French lyric poet. 1780–1857.

LETTERS—(chiefly familiar)—American and English.

Jefferson's (Thomas) Correspondence. See Randolph's Memoirs of Jefferson.

Adams's (John) Letters. See his Diary, etc.

† Curwin's (Samuel) Letters. See his "Journal," etc.

Ingersoll's Inchiquin Letters. About literature, politics, etc.

† Bryant's Letters from Spain, etc. Descriptive.

† Adams's (Mrs. John) Letters. 2 vols.

† Hale's (Mrs.) Library of Standard Letters. A judicious selection.

Remark.—Where the letters of any particular individual are not published by themselves—in distinct form—they will often be found interlinked with the Life; this is a favorite mode of writing biography at the present day.

"The Paston Letters." Highly interesting. Written during the reigns of Henry VI., Edward IV., Richard III., and Henry VII.

* Howell's Letters. A politician, traveller, and diplomatist. 1594–1666. Amusing and full of anecdote.

Russell's (Lady) Letters. Wife of the patriot.

* Swift's (Dean) 1667–1745. "Drapier's Letters." By Dean Swift, attacking a debased coinage introduced into Ireland. Famous in their day.

Pope's Literary Correspondence.

Chesterfield's (Lord) Letters to his Son.

Walpole's (Horace) Correspondence. 9 vols. 1718–'97. The most popular of all his writings.

† Gray's Letters. The poet. His letters are regarded as models of epistolary excellence. Born 1716.

Montagu's (Lady Mary Wortley) Letters. Born 1720. Mrs. Hale has edited this collection.

† Cowper's Letters. The poet. In ease and manly simplicity has never been surpassed as an epistolary writer. Born 1731.

Goldsmith's "Chinese Letters." Satirizing the civilization of the day. Born 1731.

"Junius's" Letters. Bohn's edition, with notes. The real name of the writer is not yet determined.

"Plymley's (Peter) Letters." By Sydney Smith, advocating Catholic emancipation. Rich in wit and satire, as well as in forcible argument.

† Byron's Letters. See his Life. Are admirably written, witty and sensible. Byron and Moore, like Gray, Cowper, and Southey, serve to show how well poets write prose.

† Moore's (Thomas) Letters. See Life.

* "Peter's Letters to his Kinsfolk." By Lockhart. Pictures of Scottish character.

"Paul's Letters to his Kinsfolk." By Sir Walter Scott. Amusing sketches of persons and sights at Paris after the Restoration, but prejudiced and often inaccurate.

Wellington (Duke of), Selection from his Correspondence. By Col. Gurwood.

Collingwood's (Admiral Lord) Letters and Journal.

* Cornwallis (Miss Caroline F.), Selections from the Letters of. This wonderfully-gifted woman was author of "Small Books on Great Subjects," etc.

* Ellis's Letters of Eminent Literary Men. Edition of 1848. Illustrative of English history, etc., with notes. They are much esteemed.

Lowe's (Sir Hudson) Letters and Journal. Edited by Forsyth. This publication might be read along with O'Meara's Napoleon in Exile.

"The Greyson Letters." Now well known to be the production of H. Rogers.

† "Literature in Letters." Composed of selections by J. P. Holcombe.

LETTERS—Foreign.

Cicero's Epistles. 107–43 B. C. In Harper's Classical Library.

Pliny the Younger's Epistles. 61–113 A. D. Harper's or Bohn's Classical Library.

Petrarch's Letters. The Italian poet. Born 1304.

"The Provincial Letters." By Pascal, in support of Arnauld, a Jansenist, in his controversy with the Sorbonne. Born 1623.

† Sévigné's (Madame de) Letters. Nothing can exceed the grace and naturalness of this lady's epistolary style. Born 1626.

Voltaire's Letters. Born 1694. His polished, satiric wit has, perhaps, never been equalled.

Goethe's (born 1749) "Correspondence with Schiller." "Letters to a Leipsic Friend." Edited by Otto Jahn. "Letters to a Child." The letters are chiefly by the "Child," Bettine Brentano.

Mozart's Letters. Born 1756. Translated by Lady Wallace.

Humboldt's (W.) "Letters to a Lady Friend." Display an excellent mind and heart.

Bonaparte's "Confidential Correspondence with his Brother Joseph." "Letters and Dispatches."

Perthe's Correspondence. Born 1772. An eminent German publisher. His correspondents included most of the distinguished literary men of his day.

† Mendelssohn's Letters. "Bright, piquant, genial, and affectionate."—*North American Review.*

Guérin's (Maurice de) Letters.

Beethoven's Letters. Translated by Lady Wallace.

XIII.—NOVELS, ROMANCES, AND TALES.

Although I give below a list of Works of Fiction quite formidable from its length, I am far indeed from recommending the perusal of all, or even a twentieth part, to my readers. The reasons for making the list so long have been chiefly a wish to consult the needs of persons subscribing to libraries, and a desire to furnish parents, etc., with a list of novels which will enable them promptly to decide upon the fitness or unfitness of any book of the kind presented by young persons for their approval. In such cases, if this book is not found in this list, or if belonging to the inferior class (No. 4), I would venture, at the risk of being deemed presumptuous, to suggest an examination of the book before giving sanction to its perusal.

If many popular and unobjectionable works are omitted, it is because I have endeavored to select those that were not merely harmless, but meritorious, excepting the fourth class. In novels, as in poetry, it is a waste of time to read any but the best—a taste for the best, be it understood, *can be cultivated.* It only requires a little self-denial for a time, and the patient perusal of a few good models. This simple experiment will teach all, save the hopelessly dull or the incurably tasteless, that fictions of the higher order yield even greater enjoyment than their unworthy rivals, not to mention the decided gain in mental culture and in information.

In order to assist the inexperienced reader in making some discrimination in his choice, I have divided all the novelists whose names are given into four classes, number one denoting those of the first rank; numbers two, three, and four, denoting a corresponding descent in the scale of merit. It must be premised that this division is quite arbitrary; between individual writers in the same class there is often a wide difference. In the distribution, and occasional brief notices, I have followed the best critics. It is possible that some names of repute, either of native authors of fiction or of transatlantic authors *republished* in this country, have been overlooked; the oversight, if chargeable, will be viewed indulgently when the vast array of novel literature, increasing at a rate somewhat greater than four hundred novels a year, is considered. The productions of distinguished novelists are generally given in chronological order, with an attempt at marking the epochs in style, treatment, etc., by giving date of publication. Many of the older novels cited are out of print, but may be had in the chief public libraries:

About (Edmond F.) 2d cl. (French).
Tolla: a Tale of Modern Rome.
Germanie.
The Man with the Broken Ear.

The latter is a very clever political squib. About has also written: Les Mariages de Paris, Le Roi des Montagnes, etc., besides dramas, political works, etc., with great success; but I am not aware that they are translated.

Aguilar (Grace). 2d class.
Home Influence.
Mother's Recompense.
Days of Bruce. 2 vols.
Home Scenes and Heart Studies.
Woman's Friendship.
Women of Israel. 2 vols.
Vale of Cedars.

A writer of great purity and tenderness.

Aide (Hamilton). 3d class.
Carr of Carrlyon.

Ainsworth (W. H.) 3d class.
Crichton.
Windsor Castle.
Guy Fawkes.
The Tower of London.
Old Saint Paul's.

Ainsworth's early novels are quite inferior—vulgar in tone and in subjects.

Andersen (Hans Christian). 2d cl.
The Improvisatore.
O. T.
Only a Fiddler.
Picture-Book, etc.
Tales. 3 series.
The Two Baronesses.

The Improvisatore has many beautiful and life-like pictures of Italy. The last on the list is descriptive of Danish society. The Tales are Andersen's most popular productions.

Auerbach (Berthold). 1st class.
On the Heights.
Tales of the Black Forest.
Edelweiss.
The Barefooted Maiden.
Our Villa on the Rhine.
Villa Eden.

Austen (Jane). 1st class.
Sense and Sensibility.
Pride and Prejudice.
Mansfield Park.
Emma.
Persuasion.
Northanger Abbey.
Noted for truthful description and delicate delineation of character. Sir Walter Scott considered Miss Austen unequalled, as a novelist, in this latter respect.

Ballantyne (R. M.) 3d class.
The Gorilla-Hunters.

Balzac (H. de). 1st class.
Eugénie Grandet.
Père Goriot.
The Alchemist.
César Birotteau.
Petty Annoyances of Married Life.
Generally considered to stand at the head of French classic novelists.

Banim (J.) 3d class.
The Smuggler.
The Ghost-Hunter.
Tales of the O'Hara Family.
The Mayor of Windgap.
Canvassing.
The two last-named are inferior.

Barham (Rev. R. H.) 2d class.
The Ingoldsby Legends.
A series of humorous stories in verse.

"Barry Gray." 2d class.
My Married Life at Hill-side.
Cakes and Ale at Woodbine.

Biernatski. 3d class.
The Hallig; or, The Sheepfold in the Waters.
Translated by Mrs. Marsh. Has a religious tendency.

Bird (Dr. R. M.) 3d class.
Nick of the Woods.
Has written two other novels of little merit.

Björnsen. 2d class.
The Fisher Maiden.
Arne: Happy Boy.
Both of great beauty.

Blessington (Lady). 4th class.
Strathern.
Confessions of an Elderly Lady, etc.
Governess.
Marmaduke Herbert.
Victims of Society.

Borrow (G.) 2d class.
Lavengro.
The Romany Rye. (Sequel.)

Braddon (Miss M. E.) 3d class.
Birds of Prey.
Charlotte's Inheritance.
Dead Sea Fruit.
Lady Audley's Secret.
John Marchmont's Legacy.
Darrell Markham.
Eleanor's Victory, etc., etc.
A sensational writer. The first three novels evince much improvement upon her early productions.

Bremer (Fredrika). 2d class.
Neighbors.
President's Daughter.
H—— Family.
Home; or, Family Cares, etc.
Nina. (Sequel to President's Daughter.)
Sketches of Every-day Life.
Brothers and Sisters.
Father and Daughter.
Four Sisters.
Life in Dalecarlia.
Midnight Sun.
New Sketches of Every-day Life.
Parsonage of Mora.
Easter Offering.
Give some graphic pictures of Swedish and German Life, and have an excellent tone pervading them.

Brontè (Anne). 2d class.

The Tenant of Wildfell Hall.

Brontè (Charlotte). 1st class.

Jane Eyre. Villette.
Shirley. The Professor.

Brontè (Emily). 2d class.

Wuthering Heights.

The rare merit of these three sisters is universally acknowledged, especially the originality and descriptive power of Charlotte. The novels of the two other sisters verge occasionally on the horrible, and all are sometimes coarse.

Brooke (Henry). 2d class.

Fool of Quality.

Has stood the test of a century and upward. Charles Kingsley has edited a new edition.

Brooks (Shirley). 2d class.

Aspen Court. Gordian Knot.
Silver Cord. Sooner or Later.

Brown (Charles Brockden). 2d cl.

Edgar Huntley. Clara Howard.
Wieland. Jane Talbot.
Arthur Merwyn. Ormond.

An able American novelist.

Brown (John). 3d class.

Julia of Baiæ.

Illustrative of ancient Italian history.

Brunton (Mrs. Mary). 2d class.

Self-Control. Emmeline.

An old standard author.

Bulwer (Edw.) (Lord Lytton). 1st cl.

Falkland (1827). Last Days of Pompeii.
Pelham. Rienzi.
Disowned. Leila.
Devereux. Calderon.
Paul Clifford. Godolphin.
Ernest Maltravers. Night and Morning.
Alice; or, the Mysteries. Zanoni (1842).
Eugene Aram. Last of the Barons
Student. Harold.
Pilgrims of the Rhine. Lucretia.
Caxtons (1850). My Novel.
What will He Do with It? Strange Story. (1861.)

The above list, with two or three exceptions, is in the order of publication. The Caxtons and My Novel are considered Bulwer's best. Rienzi and the Last Days of Pompeii are fine specimens of the historical novel.

Bulwer (Lady). 3d class.

Cheveley; or, the Man of Honor.

Burney (Frances) (Mme. D'Arblay). 2d class.

Evelina (1778). Cecilia.
Camilla.

Evelina produced much sensation when first published.

Cary (Alice). 3d class.

Clovernook. Married, not Mated.

Carlen (Emilie). 2d class.

Ivar.
Lover's Stratagem.
The Brothers' Bet.
Whimsical Woman.
One Year.
Birthright.
Marie Louise.
Bride of Omberg.
John; or, a Cousin, etc.
Gustavus Lindorm.
Home in the Valley.

Is much admired, here and in Europe.

Carleton (William). 2d class.

Traits and Stories of the Irish Peasantry.
Fardarougha, the Miser.
Jane Sinclair.
Valentine McClutchy.

The first two on the list his best.

Cervantes. 1st class.

Don Quixote.

For more than three centuries has delighted readers of all ages and of every class.

Chamier (Capt.) 2d class.

Ben Brace.
Life of a Sailor.

Unfortunate Man.

Once very popular.

Chamisso (A. von). 2d class.

Peter Schlemihl.

A celebrated and amusing story of a man who lost his shadow.

"Charlotte Elizabeth" (Mrs. Tonna). 3d class.

Helen Fleetwood.
Judah's Lion.
Siege of Derry.
Alice Bender, etc.
Flowers of Innocence.
Fortune-Teller, etc.
Glimpses of the Past.
Judæa Capta.
Passing Thoughts.
Philip and his Garden.
Rockite: an Irish Story.
Tales for the Young.

Of a moral tendency.

Chateaubriand. 2d class.

Atala. The Martyrs.

The first is a story of early Indian life in America; the second illustrates early Christian history.

Chatrian. (*See* Erckmann.)

Chubbuck (Emily) ("Fanny Forester"). 3d class.

Alderbrook.
Trippings in Author-Land.

Clark (Mary Cowden). 2d class.

Iron Cousin.

Cockton (Henry). 3d class.

Valentine Vox. Percy Effingham.
Stanley Thorn. Sylvester Sound.

Collins (Wilkie). 1st class.

Antonina. Dead Secret.
Basil. Woman in White.
Hide and Seek. No Name.
After Dark. Armadale.
Queen of Hearts. Moonstone.

Collins is a master in the art of developing sensation and mystery. On the better side, he possesses a good English style, and fine descriptive power.

Conscience (H.) 2d class.

Sketches of Flemish Life.
The Lion of Flanders, etc., etc.

Cooke (John Esten). 3d class.

Henry St. John.
Leather Stocking and Silk.
Virginia Comedians.
Surry of Eagle's Nest.

Cooper (James Fenimore). 1st cl.

Precaution. [1811.]
Spy. [1821.]
Pioneers (4).
Pilot (*s*).
Lionel Lincoln.
Last of the Mohicans (3).
Prairie (5). [1827.]
Red Rover (*s*).
Wept of the Wish-ton-Wish.
Water-Witch (*s*).
Bravo. [1832.]
Heidenmauer.
Headsman of Berne.
Monikins.
Homeward Bound.
Home as Found. (Sequel.)
Pathfinder (2). [1840.]
Mercedes of Castile.
Deerslayer (1).
Two Admirals (*s*).
Wing and Wing (*s*).
Wyandotte.
Ned Myers.
Afloat and Ashore (*s*).
Miles Wallingford (*s*). (Sequel.)
Satanstoe (*a*). [1845.]
Chainbearer (*b*).
Red Skins (*c*).
Crater; or, Vulcan's Peak (*s*).
Oak Openings.
Jack Tar (*s*).
Sea Lions (*s*).
Ways of the Hour.

In the list the order of publication is followed. The novels marked (1), (2), (3), (4), (5), form the Leather Stocking Series; those marked (*a*), (*b*), (*c*), the Little Page Series; and those with (*s*), the Sea Tales. The Spy, Leather Stocking, and Sea Tales, with some exceptions among the latter, are Cooper's most admired novels.

Cottin (Madame). 2d class.

Elizabeth; or, the Exiles of Siberia.

Craik (Miss G. M.) 3d class.

Lost and Won.
Leslie Tyrrell.
Winifred's Wooing.
Mildred.

Craven (Mrs. A.) 2d class.

A Sister's Story.

First published in France, where it acquired a great reputation.

Croker (T. Crofton). 3d class.

Fairy Legends of the South of Ireland.
Barney Mahoney, etc., etc.

Croly (Rev. Dr. Geo.) 2d class.

Salathiel.

Founded on the ancient legend of the Wandering Jew. A brilliant composition.

Cummings (Miss M.) 3d class.

Lamplighter. El Fureides.
Mabel Vaughan. Haunted Hearts.

Cupples (Geo.) 2d class.

The Green Hand.
The Two Frigates.

From Blackwood's Magazine.

Curtis (Geo. W.) 2d class.

Trumps.

Dasent (G. W.) 2d class.

Popular Tales from the Norse.
Story of Burnt Njal.
Story of Gisli the Outlaw.

Defoe (Daniel). 1st class.

Robinson Crusoe.

De Mille. 2d class.

Cord and Creese.
The Lady of the Ice.

De Staël (Baroness). 1st class.

Delphine. Corinne.

De Vigny (Count A.) 2d class.

Cinq-Mars.

De Witt (Madame). 2d class.

A French Country Family.

Dickens (Charles). 1st class.

Pickwick-Club Papers. [1837.]
Nicholas Nickleby.
Oliver Twist.
Old Curiosity Shop.
Barnaby Rudge.
Martin Chuzzlewit. [1842.]
Dombey and Son.
David Copperfield.
Bleak House.
Hard Times.
Little Dorrit.
Tale of Two Cities.
Great Expectations.
Our Mutual Friend.
Edwin Drood.

Short Stories.

Cricket on the Hearth.
The Chimes.
Battle of Life.
Christmas Carol.
Haunted Man.
Lamplighter's Story.
House to Let.
Mrs. Lirriper's Legacy.
Uncommercial Traveller.
Wife's Story.
Mugby Junction.
No Thoroughfare (in part), etc.

David Copperfield, the Pickwick Papers, Barnaby Rudge, and Martin Chuzzlewit, are generally considered Dickens's ablest productions, but for widely different reasons. Dickens's early Christmas stories are also truly exquisite; in them, as in the novels, we may discern a fine poetic faculty. In fact, many passages might be pointed out, which, rarely needing the change of a syllable, in sentiment and *versification*, have all the spirit and ring of genuine poetry. The Appletons publish a remarkably cheap edition of Dickens.

Disraeli (Benjamin). 1st class.

Vivian Grey. [1827.]
The Young Duke.
Contarini Fleming.
Alroy.

Henrietta Temple.
Venetia.
Coningsby.
Sybil.
Tancred.
Lothair.

The last four novels were written since Disraeli entered into political life, and have politics more or less mingled with the plot. The Appletons publish a cheap edition.

Drury (Miss A. H.) 2d class.

Eastbury.
Misrepresentation.
Light and Shade.
Deep Waters.
Friends and Fortune.

Dupuy (Miss E. A.) 3d class.

Country Neighborhood.
Planter's Daughter.

Edgeworth (Maria). 1st class.

Novels. 10 vols.
Frank. 2 vols.
Harry and Lucy. 2 vols.
Moral Tales. 2 vols.
Popular Tales. 2 vols.
Rosamond.

Of the novels, Helen, Castle Rackrent, and The Absentee, are the best. Miss Edgeworth is held in high esteem as a writer for the young.

Edwards (Amelia B.) 3d class.

Barbara's History.
Ladder of Life.
My Brother's Wife.
Hand and Glove.
Half a Million of Money.
Miss Carew.

Edwards (Mrs. Annie). 2d class.

Archie Lovell.
Stephen Lawrence.
Susan Fielding.

Edwards (H. S.) 3d class.

The Three Louisas.

Eichendorff. 2d class.

Good for Nothing.

"Eliot, George" (Mrs. G. H. Lewes). 1st class.

Scenes of Clerical Life. [1857.]
Adam Bede.
Mill on the Floss.
Silas Marner. [1861.]
Romola. [1863.]
Felix Holt, the Radical. [1866.]

The critics pronounce Silas Marner and Romola her finest intellectual efforts.

Ellis (Mrs.) 3d class.

Chapters on Wives.
Home; or, The Iron Rule.
Look to the End.
Dangers of Dining Out.
Minister's Family.
Pretension.
Self-Deception.
Somerville Hall.
Temper and Temperament.

Eötvos (J.) 2d class.

The Carthusian.
The Notary.

The latter is particularly admired for its descriptive power.

Erckmann-Chatrian. 2d class.

A Peasant's Story.
Madame Thérèse; or, The Volunteer.
The Conscript of 1813.
Story of the Invasion of 1814.
Waterloo. (Sequel to Conscript.)
The Blockade, etc.

At the present date (Jan., 1870), all the above have not appeared in English.

Evans (Augusta) (Mrs. Wilson). 3d class.

Beulah.
Macaria.
St. Elmo.
Inez.
Vashti.

Fay (Theodore). 2d class.

Norman Leslie.

Ferrier (Miss). 2d class.

Inheritance.
Destiny.
Marriage.

Highly praised by Sir Walter Scott.

Feuillet (Octave). 2d class.
Sybille.
Romance of a Poor Young Man.

"Forester (Fanny)."
See Chubbuck.

Fouqué (De la Motte). 1st class.
Sintram.
Undine.
Thiodolf, the Icelander.
A singularly charming writer.

Fraser (James B.) 2d class.
The Kuzzilbash.
An excellent delineator of Oriental life and character.

Freytag (Gustav). 1st class.
Debit and Credit.
The Lost Manuscript.
Has attained a signal success here as well as abroad.

Fullerton (Lady G.) 3d class.
Grantley Manor.
A Stormy Life.
Too Strange Not to be True.
Lady Bird.

Fullom (S. W.) 2d class.
The Daughter of Night.
The Great Highway, etc., etc.

Galt (John). 2d class.
Annals of the Parish.
Entail.
Provost.
Laurie Todd.
Adam Blair.
Ayrshire.
Last of the Lairds.
Mansie Wauch.
Rengan Gilhaize.
Rothelan.
Sir Andrew Wylie.
Southenan.
Spae Wife.
Steamboat.
Galt has never been surpassed in depicting middle-class Scotch life.

Gaskell (Mrs.) 2d class.
Mary Barton. [1848.]
Moorland Cottage.
Ruth. [1853.]
North and South.
Cranford.
Lizzie Leigh.
My Lady Ludlow.
Right at Last.
Sylvia's Lovers.
Cousin Phillis.
Wives and Daughters.
Nos. 1 and 3 are perhaps the best specimens of Mrs. Gaskell's powers.

Gerstaecker (F.) 2d class.
How a Bride was Won, etc.
Wanderings of German Emigrants.
The Feathered Arrow.
The Two Convicts.

Girardin (Madame de). 3d class.
Marguerite.
Stories of an Old Maid.

Gleig (Rev. G. L.) 2d class.
Subaltern.
Chelsea Prisoners.
Light Dragoon.
Country Curate.

Godwin (W.) 2d class.
Caleb Williams. [1794 and 1870.]
Deloraine.
St. Leon, etc.
The first is by far his best novel.

Goethe (J. W. von). 1st class.
Sorrows of Werther. [1774.]
Elective Affinities.
Wilhelm Meister.
The New Paris.
The Tale. (Das Märchen.)

Goldsmith (Oliver). 1st class.
The Vicar of Wakefield.

Gore (Mrs.) 3d class.
Cecil.
The Banker's Wife.
Peers and Parvenus.
The Birthright.
The Royal Favorite.
The Queen of Denmark.
The Cabinet Minister.

Castles in the Air.
The Dean's Daughter.
Mrs. Armytage.
Percy; or, Fortune's Frolics.
The Tuileries, etc., etc.

Mrs. Gore's forte lay in the description of fashionable life.

Grant (James). 2d class.

Scottish Cavalier.
Jane Seaton.
Arthur Blane.
Bothwell.
Yellow Frigate.
Harry Ogilvie.
Adventures of an Aide-de-Camp.
Romance of War.
Captain of the Guard.
Philip Rollo.
Frank Hilton.
Oliver Ellis.
Highlanders of Glen Ora.
Mary of Lorraine.
Lucy Arden.
Legends of the Black Watch.

Gray. (See "Barry Gray.")

Grattan (T. C.) 3d class.

Heiress of Bruges.
Jacqueline of Holland.
Traits of Travel.

"Greenwood (Grace)." 2d class.

Stories and Legends of Travel, etc.
Stories from Various Ballads, etc.

Greenwood (James). 2d class.

The Little Ragamuffin.
Reuben Davidger.

Grey (Mrs.) 3d class.

The Gambler's Wife.
The Bosom Friend.
The Young Husband.

Griffin (Gerald). 2d class.

The Collegians.
Tales of the Munster Festivals: Card-Drawing. Half-Sir. Suil-Dhuv, the Coiner.
Duke of Monmouth.
Rivals.

Describes ably Irish character. The first two on the list the best.

Guerazzi (F. D.) 2d class.

Battle of Benevento.
Isabella Orsini.
Beatrice Cenci.

Political in their tendency, and of great power and beauty.

Guizot (Madame). 3d class.

Young Student.

Hale (Mrs. Sarah J.) 3d class.

Liberia.
Sketches of American Character.
Traits of American Life.

Haliburton (T. C.) 3d class.

Clockmaker.
Nature and Human Nature.
Old Judge.
Sam Slick.

Hall (Mrs. S. C.) 2d class.

Lights and Shadows of Irish Character.
Stories of the Irish Peasantry.
Midsummer Eve.
Can Right be Wrong?
Harry O'Reardon.
Whiteboy.
Tales of Woman's Trials.

Nos. 1, 2, and 3, are most admired, particularly No. 3.

Hamilton (Captain T.) 2d class.

Cyril Thornton.

Hamilton (Mrs. Elizabeth). 3d cl.

The Cottagers of Glenburnie.

A story of humble Scotch life.

Hannay (James). 2d class.

Singleton Fontenoy.

Able and interesting.

Hardenberg (F. von). 3d class.

Henry of Ofterdingen.

"Harland (Marion)" (Mrs. Terhune). 3d class.

Nemesis.
Moss Side.
Hidden Path.
Alone.
Miriam.
Colonel Floyd's Wards.
Husbands and Homes.
Husks.

Haven (Alice B.) ("Cousin Alice"). 3d class.

The Coopers. Loss and Gain.
Home Stories.

Hawthorne (Nathaniel). 1st class.

Twice-Told Tales. [1837.]
Mosses from an Old Manse.
The Scarlet Letter. [1850.]
House of the Seven Gables.
Snow Image; and other Twice-Told Tales.
Blithedale Romance.
Marble Faun. [1860.]

"Distinguished for the finish of his style and the delicacy of his psychological insight."

Hentz (Caroline Lee). 4th class.

Aunt Patty's Scrap Bag.
Rena; or, the Snow-Bird.
Marcus Warland.
Ernest Linwood.
Linda.
Robert Graham. (Sequel.)
Banished Son.
Planter's Northern Bride.
Eoline.
Love after Marriage.
Helen and Arthur.
Lost Daughter.

Herbert (H. W.) 3d class.

Cavaliers of England.
Chevaliers of France.
The Brothers.
Cromwell.
Knights of England and France.
Marmaduke Wyvil.
Roman Traitor.
Wager of Battle.

Heyse (Paul). 2d class.

L'Arrabiata and other Tales.
The Lonely One. (Published in same volume with Magdalena.)

Hoffman (C. Fenno). 2d class.

Greyslaer.

Hoffmann (E. T. W.) 2d class.

"Strange Stories."

Wonderful, but fantastic.

Hofland (Mrs.) 4th class.

Son of a Genius. Self-Denial.
Czarina. Sisters.
Decision. Tales of the Manor.
Energy. Unloved One.
Integrity. Young Pilgrim.
Moderation.
Reflection.

The novels of this amiable lady, excellent as they are in tendency, are superseded by others better in every respect.

Hogg (James). 2d class.

Winter Evening Tales.
Shepherd's Calendar.
Siege of Roxburgh.
Tales of the Wars of Montrose.
Three Perils of Women.
Tales and Sketches.
The Brownie of Bodsbeck, etc.

Abound in humor and life-like description.

Holmes (Dr. O. W.) 1st class.

The Autocrat of the Breakfast-Table.
Professor at the Breakfast-Table.
Elsie Venner.
The Guardian Angel.

Evince shrewd perception of character, delicate wit, with decided originality.

Holmes (Mrs. Mary J.) 4th class.

Darkness and Daylight.
Marian Grey.
Rose Mather.
Cousin Maud, etc.
Dora Deane.
English Orphans.
Homestead on the Hillside.
Hugh Worthington.
Lena Rivers.
Maggie Miller.
Meadow Brook.
Tempest and Sunshine.

Of slight repute as a novelist.

Hood (Thomas). 2d class.

Tylney Hall.

Hood's true field was poetry.

Hook (Theodore E.) 2d class.

Maxwell.
Gilbert Gurney.
Sayings and Doings.
All in the Wrong.
Ned Musgrave.
Parson's Daughter.
Jack Brag.
Love and Pride, etc., etc.

The first three novels on the list are considered Hook's best. There are several series of Sayings and Doings. Gilbert Gurney is a kind of autobiography of Hook.

Howard (Edward). 3d class.

Outward Bound.
Ratlin the Reefer.
The Old Commodore.
Jack Ashore, etc.

Hardly maintains his old popularity.

Howitt (Mrs. Mary). 3d class.

Alice Franklin.
Author's Daughter.
Dial of Love.
Heir of Nast Wayland.
Hope On, Hope Ever.
Little Coin, Much Care.
Love and Money.
My Own Story.
My Uncle the Clockmaker.
Sowing and Reaping.
Stories of the Reformation.
Strive and Thrive.
Two Apprentices.
Which is the Wiser ?
Who shall be Greatest ?
Wood Leighton.

Adapted chiefly for the young, and of unequal merit.

Howitt (William). 3d class.

Jack of the Mill.
Man of the People.
Tallangetta.

Hughes (T.) 2d class.

Tom Brown's School Days.
Scouring of the White Horse.
Tom Brown at Oxford.

An agreeable, manly writer. The second novel is not so popular as the others.

Hugo (Victor). 1st class.

Hunchback of Notre-Dame. [1831.]
Les Misérables. [1862.]
The Toilers of the Sea.
The Man Who Laughs.

Hugo's novels are distinguished for the power and dramatic force with which they handle social questions.

Hungerford (James). 3d class.

The Old Plantation.

Inchbald (Mrs.) 2d class.

A Simple Story.
Nature and Art.

Two old classics, still admired.

Ingraham (J. H.) 3d class.

Burton ; or, The Sieges.
Lafitte, the Pirate.
Montezuma.
Pillar of Fire.
Prince of the House of David.
Sunny South.
Throne of David.

Irving (Washington). 1st class.

Sketch Book. [1816.]
Bracebridge Hall. [1822.]
Tales of a Traveller.
The Alhambra. [1832.]
Legends of Spain.
Woolfert's Roost.

For other light works of Irving's, see under "Miscellaneous."

James (G. P. R.) 2d class.

Agincourt (*b*).
Agnes Sorel (*b*).
Aims and Obstacles.
Ancient Régime.
Arabella Stuart (*b*).
Arrah Neil (*b*).
Attila.
Beauchamp.
Castle of Ehrenstein.
Cavalier.
Charles Tyrrel.
The Commissioner.
The Convict.

Corse de Leon.
Darnley (*b*).
De Lorme.
Desultory Man.
False Heir.
Fate.
Forest Days (*b*).
Gentlemen of the Old School.
Gypsy.
Gowrie.
Heidelberg.
Henry Masterton.
Henry of Guise.
Henry Smeaton.
Huguenot.
Jacqueric.
John Marston Hall.
King's Highway.
Last of the Fairies.
Leonora d'Orco.
Lord Montagu's Page.
Man-at-Arms.
Man in Black.
Margaret Graham.
Mary of Burgundy.
Morley Ernstein (*b*).
Old Dominion.
Old Oak Chest.
One of a Thousand.
Pequinillo.
Philip Augustus.
Richelieu (*b*).
Robber.
Rose d'Albret (*b*).
Russell.
Sir Theodore Broughton.
Smuggler.
Step-Mother.
Story without a Name.
String of Pearls.
Tales, etc., of the Passions.
Thirty Years Since.
Ticonderoga.
Whim and its Consequences.
Woodman.

James's novels have all a strong family likeness, and are often tedious, but they have many good points, and, at least, are far preferable to the vulgar sensational. A (*b*) denotes the best.

Jeaffreson (J. C.) 2d class.
Isabel.
Live it Down.
Not Dead Yet.
Olive Blake's Good Work.
Has some superior claims.

Jenkin (Mrs. W. C.) 3d class.
Who Breaks, Pays.
A Psyche of To-Day.

Jerrold (Douglas). 2d class.
Story of a Feather.
Chronicles of Clovernook.
Very pleasant light reading.

Jewsbury (Geraldine E.) 3d class.
Constance Herbert.
History of an Adopted Child, etc.

Johnson (Dr. Samuel). 2d class.
Rasselas.
A beautiful and time-honored romance.

Kavanagh (Julia). 3d class.
Dora.
Nathalie (*b*).
Grace Lee.
Rachel Gray (*b*).
Adele.
Beatrice.
Daisy Burns.
Madeleine (*b*).
Queen Mab.
Seven Years, etc.
Sybil's Second Love.
Silvia.
A graceful and admired writer. A (*b*) indicates some of her best novels.

Kennedy (John P.) 2d class.
Horseshoe Robinson.
Rob of the Bowl.
Swallow Barn.
A standard American novelist.

Kennedy (Grace). 4th class.
Anna Ross.
Father Clement.
Philip Colville.
Abbey of Innismoyle.
The Decision.
Dunallan.

Kimball (R. B.) 2d class.
Romance of Student Life, etc.
Saint Leger.

Under-Currents.
Was He Successful?

The superior merit of the above novels is well known. They are marked by good taste and naturalness.

Kingsley (Rev. Charles). 1st class.
Alton Locke. [1849.]
Yeast.
Hypatia. [1853.]
Voyages, etc., of Sir Amyas Leigh.
Westward Ho!
Two Years Ago.
Hereward.

Of unusual vigor and graphic power.

Kingsley (Henry). 2d class.
Ravenshoe.
Austin Elliot.
Jeoffrey Hamlyn.
The Hillyars and the Burtons.
Leighton Court.
Silcote of Silcotes.
Stretton.

Kirkland (Mrs. C. M.) 3d class.
Forest Life.
New Home, etc.
Western Clearings.

Lamartine (A. de). 2d class.
Raphael.
Memoirs of my Youth.
Genevieve.

Landon (Miss). 3d class.
Ethel Churchill.
Romance and Reality.

Inferior to her poetic pieces.

Laurence (George). 2d class.
Guy Livingstone.
Sword and Gown.
Barren Honor.
Border and Bastile.
Maurice Dering.
Held in Bondage.
Brakespeare.
Sans Merci.
Breaking a Butterfly.

A writer of no mean distinction, but disfigured by certain faults.

"Lee, Holme." (Miss Parr.) 2d cl.
Basil Godfrey's Caprice.
Against Wind and Tide.
Warp and Woof.
Kathie Brand.
Sylvan Holt's Daughter.

Steadily advancing in reputation.

Lee (Sophia). 2d class.
Kruitzner.

Inspired Byron's Werner.

Lee (Misses H. and S.) 2d class.
Canterbury Tales.

Standard productions of their class.

Le Fanu (J. S.) 2d class.
Uncle Silas.
Guy Deverell.
All in the Dark.
The Tenants of Mallory.
A Lost Name.

A powerful but sensational writer.

Lemon (Mark). 2d class
Wait for the End.
Loved at Last.
Golden Fetters, etc.

Le Sage. 1st class.
Gil Blas.

Lever (Charles). 2d class.
Harry Lorrequer.
Charles O'Malley.
Tom Burke of Ours.
Roland Cashel.
The Knight of Gwynne.
Davenport Dunn.
Arthur O'Leary.
Barrington.
Confessions of Con Cregan.
Daltons.
Day's Ride.
Fortunes of Glencoe.
Gerald Fitzgerald.
Horace Templeton.
Jack Hinton.
Kate O'Donoghue.
Luttrell of Arran.
Martins of Cro' Martin.
Maurice Tiernay.

One of Them.
Sir Jasper Carew.
Tony Butler.
Sir Brook Fosbrooke.
That Boy of Norcott's.
Bramleighs of Bishop's Folly.

The first seven on the list may be regarded as examples of Lever's best.

Lewes (G. H.) 2d class.

Three Sisters and Three Fortunes.

By the versatile author of Goethe's Life, etc., etc.

Lockhart (John G.) 2d class.

Valerius.
Reginald Dalton.
Matthew Wald.

The first—an historical novel—is perhaps the best.

Longfellow (Henry W.) 2d class.

Hyperion. Kavanagh.

Display a poetic refinement.

Longstreet (A. B.) 3d class.

Georgia Scenes.

Lover (Samuel). 3d class.

Legends and Stories of Ireland.
Handy Andy.
Barney O'Reirdon.
Rory O'More.
£ s. d.; or, Treasure Trove.
Tom Crosbie and his Friends.

McDonald (George). 2d class.

Guild Court.
Alec Forbes.
Annals of a Quiet Neighborhood.
Seaboard Parish. (Sequel.)

A writer of distinguished merit.

McCarthy (Justin). 2d class.

Paul Massie.
Waterdale Neighbors.
My Enemy's Daughter.

Mackenzie (Henry). 3d class.

Man of Feeling.
Man of the World.

Have lost much of their old fame.

Mackenzie (Dr. Shelton). 2d class.

Tressilian and his Friend.

MacIntosh (Maria J.) 3d class.

Charms and Counter-Charms.
Evenings at Donaldson Manor.
Meta Gray.
Aunt Kitty's Tales.
Conquest and Self-Conquest.
Lofty and Lowly.
Praise and Principle.
Two Lives.
Two Pictures.
Violet; or, Cross and Crown.
Woman an Enigma.

Admirable in tone, but deficient in power.

Manzoni (Alessandro). 2d class.

The Betrothed. (I Promessi Sposi.)

A celebrated production.

Marlitt (E.) 2d class.

Old Mam'selle's Secret.
Gold Elsie.
Countess Gisela.
Over Yonder.
Magdalena.

A very pleasing and much admired writer.

Marryat (Captain F.) 2d class.

Frank Mildmay. [1830.]
Midshipman Easy.
Peter Simple.
Jacob Faithful.
Japhet in Search of a Father.
Masterman Ready.
Children of the New Forest.
Diary of a Blasé.
King's Own.
Little Savage.
Mission; or, Scenes in Africa.
Monsieur Violet.
Newton Forster.
Pacha of Many Tales
Percival Keene.
Phantom Ship.
Pirate and Three Cutters.
Poacher.
Poor Jack.
Privateersman.
Sea-King.
Settlers in Canada.

Snarleyow.

Valerie, etc.

A manly, natural, and amusing writer. The *last* nine novels are not equal, as a rule, to the others. There is a cheap edition of Marryat issued by the Appletons.

Marryat (Miss Florence). 3d class.

Veriniqui.

Marsh (Mrs.) 2d class.

The Wilmingtons.

Lettice Arnold.

Heiress of Haughton.

Adelaide Lindsay.

Aubery.

Castle Avon.

Emilia Wyndham.

Evelyn Marston.

Mount Sorel.

Mordaunt Hall.

Norman's Bridge.

Ravenscliffe.

Soldier of Fortune.

Tales of the Woods and Fields.

Time, the Avenger.

Triumphs of Time.

Two Old Men's Tales.

The Rose of Ashurst.

The first three and the last on the list are generally preferred.

Martineau (Miss Harriet). 2d class.

Deerbrook.

The Hour and the Man.

Settlers at Home.

Sowers not Reapers.

A Manchester Strike, etc., etc.

Are, in general, written to illustrate some principle.

Maturin (Edward). 3d class.

Bianca. Montezuma.

Maturin (Robert C.) 3d class.

Melmoth.

The Fatal Revenge, etc.

Far more successful as a tragedian.

Maxwell (W. H.) 2d class.

Wild Sports of the West.

Stories of Waterloo.

Hector O'Halloran.

Adventures of Captain Blake.

Bivouac.

Captain O'Sullivan.

Luck is Every Thing.

Wild Sports, etc., in the Highlands.

The first three on the list are most esteemed. Maxwell had good descriptive power.

Mayhew (H.) 2d class.

Mr. and Mrs. Sandboys.

The Greatest Plague of My Life.

Mayhew Brothers. 2d class.

Image of his Father.

Magic of Kindness.

Meinhold. 2d class.

Mary Schweidler, the Amber Witch.

Sidonia, the Sorceress.

Melville (Herman). 2d class.

Typee. [1846.] Redburn.

Omoo. Whitejacket. [1850.]

Mardi. Moby-Dick.

Typee, Omoo, and Mardi, have their scenes in the Pacific; they have considerable charm of style, as well as a marked freshness and originality. The others are also more or less admired.

Meredith (George). 2d class.

The Ordeal of Richard Feverel.

Shaving of Shagpat.

The latter a fanciful tale of great richness of imagination.

Mitchell (Donald G.) 2d class.

Reveries of a Bachelor.

Dream Life.

Seven Stories with Basement, etc.

Dr. Johns.

A pleasing and popular writer; of polished style and refined thought.

Mitford (Miss Mary R.) 2d class.

Our Village. Belford Regis.

Atherton. Country Stories.

Of exquisite ease and simplicity.

Moore (Dr. John). 3d class.

Zeluco. Mordaunt.

Old-fashioned, but not without merit.

Moore (Thomas, the poet). 3d class.

Epicurean.

Has lost most of its old prestige.

More (Hannah). 2d class.

Cœlebs in Search of a Wife.
Shepherd of Salisbury Plain.

Morgan (Lady). 4th class.

Wild Irish Girl.
Florence Macarthy.
O'Briens and O'Flahertys.

Morier (J.) 2d class.

Hadji Baba.
Hadji Baba in England.
Zorab the Hostage.

Mügge (Theodor). 3d class.

Afraja; or, Life, etc., in Norway.

"Mühlbach (Miss L.)" 2d class.

Joseph II. and his Court.
Frederick the Great and his Court.
Berlin and Sans-Souci.
Merchant of Berlin, etc.
Frederick the Great and his Family.
Henry VIII. and Catharine Parr.
Louisa of Prussia, etc.
Marie Antoinette and her Son.
The Daughter of an Empress.
Napoleon and the Queen of Prussia.
The Empress Josephine.
Napoleon and Blucher.
Old Fritz and the New Era.
Andreas Hofer.
Schiller and Goethe.
Prince Eugene and his Times.

Have attained a rapid and wide popularity on both sides of the Atlantic.

Mulock (Miss D. M.) 2d class.

The Ogilvies. [1850.]
Olive.
Head of the Family.
Agatha's Husband.
Avillion, and other Tales.
John Halifax, Gentleman.
Nothing New.
A Life for a Life.
Christian's Mistake.
A Noble Life.
Mistress and Maid.
Two Marriages.
Woman's Kingdom. [1869.]

John Halifax, Christian's Mistake, and the Ogilvies, are, perhaps, Miss Mulock's most admired productions. She excels in delineating home and country life.

Murray (Hon. C. A.) 2d class.

Prairie Bird.

"Novalis." [*See* Hardenberg.]

Oliphant (Mrs.) 2d class.

Passages in the Life of Mrs. Margaret Maitland. [1849.]
Chronicles of Carlingford. [1855.]
Quiet Heart.
Agnes.
Athelings.
Brownlows.
Days of My Life.
House on the Moor.
Katie Stewart.
Laird of Norlaw.
Last of the Mortimers.
Lucy Crofton.
Madonna Mary.
Miss Marjoribanks.
Perpetual Curate.
A Son of the Soil.
Minister's Wife. [1869.]
The Three Brothers, etc., etc.

Nos. 2, 3, 5, 6, and 15, are especially good. All have merit; some, merit of the highest order.

Opie (Miss). 3d class.

Simple Tales.
Tales of Real Life.
Father and Daughter.
Illustrations of Lying.
Madeline.
Tales.
Tales of the Heart.
Valentine's Eve.

Chiefly adapted for the young, and of excellent tendency.

Pardoe (Miss). 2d class.

Adopted Heir.
Jealous Wife.
Life Struggle.

Romance of the Harem.
Speculation.
Wife's Trials.

Paulding (James K.) 2d class
Book of St. Nicholas.
Dutchman's Fireside.
George Mason.
Koningsmark. (Old Times in the New World.)
Old Continental.
Puritan and his Daughter.
Tales of the Good Woman.
Westward Ho!

Pickering (Ellen). 3d class.
The Grumbler.
Who shall be Heir?
Grandfather.
Agnes Serle.
Expectant.
Fright.
Kate Walsingham.
Nat Darral.
Orphan Niece.
Poor Cousin.
Prince and Pedlar.
Quiet Husband.
Secret Foe.
Squire.

An estimable writer, but without any claims of a high order.

Ploennies (Louise von). 2d class.
The Princess Ilse.

A charming story.

Poe (Edgar A.) 2d class.
Collected Tales. 2 vols.

Often display undoubted genius, and rare analytic skill.

Poole (John). 3d class.
Little Peddlington.

Porter (Anne). 3d class.
Don Sebastian.

Porter (Jane). 2d class.
Scottish Chiefs.
Thaddeus of Warsaw.
Fast of St. Magdalen.
Pastor's Fireside.
Sir Edward Seaward's Narrative.
Village of Mariendorpt.

Radcliffe (Mrs. Ann). 2d class.
Mysteries of Udolpho.
Romance of the Forest.
Gaston de Blondeville.

Once ranked high, but possess, in reality, feeble artistic merits.

Reade (Charles). 1st class.
Peg Woffington.
Christie Johnston.
Never too Late to Mend. [1856.]
Course of True Love.
White Lies.
Cloister and the Hearth.
Clouds and Sunshine.
Good Fight, and other Tales.
Love Me Little, Love Me Long.
Very Hard Cash.
Griffith Gaunt.
Foul Play. (In part.)
Put Yourself in His Place. (1st part.)

Reid (Captain Mayne). 2d class.
Boy Hunters.
Boy Tar.
Bruin.
Bush Boys.
Plant Hunters.
Cliff Climbers. (Sequel.)
Desert Home.
Forest Exiles.
Hunter's Feast.
Hunter's Trail.
Ocean Waifs.
Osceola.
Quadroon.
Ran away to Sea.
Rifle Rangers.
Scalp Hunters.
Wild Life.
White Chief.
Wood Rangers.
Young Voyageurs.
Young Yägers.

An admirable series for young folks.

Reuter (Fritz). 3d class.
In the Year 1813.

Richardson (Samuel). 2d class.

Pamela. [1740.]

Clarissa Harlowe. [1748.]

Sir Charles Grandison. [1853.]

No. 2 is regarded as the best. They are all tedious, each extending through some half-dozen volumes. Copies are rare in this country.

Richter (Jean Paul). 1st class.

Flower, Fruit, and Thorn Pieces.

Hesperus.

Titan.

Walt and Vult.

There is stuff enough in one volume of Titan to equip a score or two of ordinary novelists.

Ritchie (Mrs. A.) 3d class.

Mimic Life.

Twin Roses.

Robinson (Mrs. Edward). 3d class.

Heloise.

Life's Discipline.

Robinson (F. W.) 2d class.

Carrie's Confession.

Christie's Faith.

Mattie Astray.

Poor Humanity.

No Man's Friend.

For Her Sake.

Ruffini (J.) 2d class.

Dr. Antonio.

Lavinia.

Lorenzo Benoni.

Paragreens in Paris.

Vincenzo.

A Quiet Nook.

Rydberg (Victor). 2d class.

Last Athenian.

A good specimen of the historical novel.

Saintine (X. B.) 1st class.

Picciola.

A touching story, exquisitely told.

Sala (George A.) 2d class.

Baddington Peerage.

Seven Sons of Mammon.

Quite Alone. (In part.)

"Sand (George)." 1st class.

Fanchon, the Cricket.

Consuelo.

Countess of Rudolstadt. (Sequel.)

Sartoris (Mrs. A. Kemble). 2d cl.

A Week in a French Country House.

Schwartz (M. Sophia). 2d class.

The Man of Birth and the Woman of the People.

Scott (Sir Walter). 1st class.

Waverley. [1814.]

Guy Mannering.

Antiquary.

Black Dwarf.

Old Mortality.

Rob Roy. [1817.]

Heart of Mid-Lothian.

Bride of Lammermoor.

Legend of Montrose.

Ivanhoe. [1819.]

Monastery.

Abbot.

Kenilworth. [1821.]

Pirate.

Fortunes of Nigel.

Peveril of the Peak.

Quentin Durward. [1823.]

St. Ronan's Well.

Redgauntlet.

Betrothed.

Talisman.

Woodstock. [1826.]

Two Drovers.

Highland Widow.

Surgeon's Daughter.

Aunt Margaret's Mirror.

Fair Maid of Perth.

Anne of Geierstein.

Count Robert of Paris.

Castle Dangerous.

The novels up to and including Ivanhoe are reckoned Scott's best. Among the succeeding ones may be particularized: Kenilworth, Fortunes of Nigel, Quentin Durward, and The Talisman. The latest novels written by Scott, when oppressed by ill-health and pecuniary troubles, are quite inferior.

The novels of Scott are also published by the Appletons in cheap form. Price, 25 cents a volume.

Scott (Michael). 2d class.

Tom Cringle's Log.
The Cruise of the Midge.
Old and good standard novels.

Sedgwick (Catherine M.) 2d cl.

Hope Leslie.
Linwoods.
Rich Poor Man, etc.
Boy of Mount Righi.
Live and Let Live.
Love Token for Children.
Married or Single.
New England Tale.
Stories for Young Persons.

Sewell (Miss E. M.) 2d class.

Amy Herbert.
Cleve Hall.
Earl's Daughter.
Experience of Life.
Glimpse of the World.
Gertrude.
Hawkestone.
Ivors.
Katharine Ashton.
Laneton Parsonage.
Margaret Percival.
Ursula.
Walter Lorimer.
Some of the above belong to a class higher than No. 2 would indicate.

Shelley (Mrs.) 2d class.

Frankenstein.
Fortunes of Perkin Warbeck.
Falkner.
The last two are much inferior to Frankenstein.

Sigourney (Mrs. Lydia H.) 3d cl.

Lucy Howard's Journal.
A graceful and meritorious writer, but deficient in force and thought.

Simms (W. Gilmore). 2d class.

Partisan.
Mellichampe.
Scout.
Katharine Walton.
Foragers.
Eutaw. (Sequel.)
Charlemont.
Beauchamp. (Sequel.)
Border Beagles.
Cassique of Kiawah.
Confessions of a Blind Heart.
Guy Rivers.
Huguenots of Florida.
Martin Faber.
Pelayo; a Story of the Goth.
Richard Hurdis.
Southward Ho!
Vasconselos.
Wigwam and Cabin.
Woodcraft.
Yemassee.

Sinclair (Catharine). 3d class.

Modern Flirtations.
Beatrice.
Lord and Lady Harcourt.
Sir Edward Graham.

Smedley (F.) 2d class.

Frank Fairlegh.
Lewis Arundel, etc.

Smith (Albert). 3d class.

Christopher Tadpole.
Story of Mont Blanc, etc.

Smith (Horace). 2d class.

Brambletye House.
The Money-mad Man.
Arthur Arundel.
Adam Browne.
Gaieties and Gravities.
Tales of the Early Ages.
Walter Colyton.
Zillah.

Southworth (Mrs. E. D.) 4th class.

Curse of Clifton.
Deserted Wife.
Discarded Daughter.
Fatal Marriage.
Gypsy's Prophecy.
Haunted Homestead.
India.
Lady of the Isle.
Lost Heiress.

Love's Labor Won.
Missing Bride.
Mother-in-Law.
Retribution.
Three Beauties.
Two Sisters.
Vivia.
Wife's Victory.

Souvestre (Emile). 2d class.
Attic Philosopher in Paris.
Leaves from a Family Journal.
Popular Legends of Brittany.

Spielhagen. 2d class.
Problematical Characters.
Through Night to Light. (Sequel.)

Spindler. 2d class.
The Jew, etc., etc.

Stephens (Ann S.) 4th class.
Fashion and Famine.
Heiress of Greenhurst.
Mary Derwent.
Old Homestead.
Rejected Wife.

Stowe (Mrs. H. B.) 2d class.
May Flower. [1849.]
Uncle Tom's Cabin. [1855.]
Nina Gordon (Dred).
Minister's Wooing. [1859.]
Agnes of Sorrento.
Pearl of Orr's Island.
Old Town Folks. [1869.]
Pink and White Tyranny.

Tautphœus (Baroness). 2d class.
Quits. Cyrilla.
The Initials. Pique.
At Odds.

A charming, natural writer. Her descriptions of Bavarian life and scenery are truly life-like.

Taylor (Bayard). 2d class.
Hannah Thurston.
John Godfrey's Fortunes.
Joseph and his Friend.

Thackeray (Miss). 3d class.
Story of Elizabeth.

Thackeray (W. M.) 1st class.
Great Hoggarty Diamond.
Barry Lyndon.
Vanity Fair. [1846.]
Pendennis. [1849.]
Henry Esmond. [1852.]
Newcomes. [1855.]
Virginians.
Lovel the Widower.
Philip.

Nos. 3, 4, and 6, are perhaps the most generally liked; but, in point of artistic skill and polish, Esmond is properly placed first.

"Thomas (Miss Annie)." 3d class.
The Dower House.
Thomas Leigh.
Dennis Donne.
On Guard.
Walter Goung.
Played Out.
Called to Account.
Playing for High Stakes.
False Colors. [1869.]

Occasionally Miss Thomas's productions may be rated still higher than above.

Tieck (Ludwig). 2d class.
The Elves.

Tonna (Mrs.) See "Charlotte Elizabeth."

Trafford (F. G.) 2d class.
George Keith.

Trollope (Anthony). 1st class.
The Warden.
Barchester Towers.
Dr. Thorne.
The Bertrams.
Three Clerks.
Castle Richmond.
Framley Parsonage.
Kellys and O'Kellys.
Orley Farm.
Small House at Allington.
Rachel Gray.
Brown, Jones, and Robinson.
Miss Mackenzie.
Belton Estate.

The Claverings.
Chronicle of Barset.
Can You Forgive Her?
Phineas Finn.
He knew He was Right. [1869.]
Ralph the Heir.
Sir Harry Hotspur.

Trollope (T. Adolphus). 2d class.
Lindisfarne Chase.
Beppo, the Conscript.

Tupper (Martin F.) 4th class.
Crock of Gold.
Heart, etc.
Twins.

Walpole (Horace). 3d class.
Castle of Otranto.

Wood (Mrs. Henry). 4th class.
Castle Wafer.
Channings.
Earle's Heirs.
East Lynn.
Foggy Night.
Gervase Gastonel.
Haunted Tower.
Heir to Ashleigh.
Lord Oakburn's Daughters.
Lost Bank Note.
Mrs. Haliburton's Troubles.
Mystery.
Runaway Match.
Shadow of Ashlydyatt.
Squire Trevlyn's Heir.
Verner's Pride.
William Allain.

Warburton (Eliot). 2d class.
Darien; or, The Merchant Prince.
Reginald Hastings.

Ward (R. P.) 2d class.
Tremaine.
Chatsworth.
De Vere.
Fielding.
Penruddock.
Stirling.

Ware (William). 2d class.
Julian; or, Scenes in Judea.
Probus; or, Rome in the Third Century.
Zenobia; or, The Fall of Palmyra.

Warner (The Misses). 3d class.
Queechy.
Wide, Wide World.
Say and Seal.
Old Helmet.
Cad Crinken.
Dollars and Cents.
Hills of Shatemuc.
Melbourne House.
Mr. Rutherford's Children.

Warren (Samuel). 2d class.
Diary of a Physician.
Merchant's Clerk, etc.
Now and Then.
Ten Thousand a Year.

Willis (N. P.) 3d class.
Paul Fane.

Wilson (John). 2d class.
Foresters.
Lights and Shadows of Scottish Life.
Martyr of Carthage.
Trials of Margaret Lindsay.

Wilson (John M.) 2d class.
Tales of the Borders.

Yates (Edmund). 2d class.
Land at Last.
Kissing the Rod.
Black Sheep.
Wrecked in Port.

Yonge (Miss). 2d class.
Beechcroft.
Ben Sylvester's Word.
Castle Builders.
Clever Woman of the Family.
The Daisy Chain (*b*).
The Trial.
Dove in the Eagle's Nest.
Dynevor Terrace (*b*).
Heartsease (*b*).
Heir of Redclyffe (*b*).
Hopes and Fears.
Kenneth.
Lances of Linwood.

Little Duke.
Richard the Fearless.
The Two Guardians.
Young Stepmother.
Friarswood Post-Office.
Stokesley Secret.
Chaplet of Pearls.
The Caged Lion, etc.

As a writer for the young, especially for girls, Miss Yonge has attained a wide and well-deserved popularity. Her best novels are indicated by a (*b*); these four works will, indeed, please readers of all ages.

Zschokke (J. H. D.) 2d class.
The Dead Guest.
Gold-Makers' Village.
Veronica.
Select Tales.

A truly sensible, eloquent writer.

NOVELS—by Anonymous Authors.

N. B.—Works by the same author are connected by a brace.

The Sacristan's Household.
{ Cometh up as a Flower.
Not Wisely, but Too Well.
Red as a Rose is She. }
The Cid.
{ St. Olave's.
Jeannie's Quiet Life.
Meta's Faith. }
Erring, yet noble.
For Better for Worse.
{ Mademoiselle Moir.
Denise.
Madame Fontenoy. }
{ Carlyon's Year.
Lost Sir Massingberd.
One of the Family. }
{ Beggar on Horseback.
Found Dead. }
Story of Elizabeth.
{ Recommended to Mercy.
Zoe's Brand. }
{ Still Waters.
Dorothy, etc., etc. }
A Whim and its Consequences.
{ Paul Ferrol.
Year after Year.
Why Paul Ferrol killed his Wife. }
Caste.
Five Hundred Pounds Reward.
Faith Gartney's Childhood.

Remark.—All the novels named above have claims, some of them high claims, on the score of talent, but a few are objectionable in point of good taste.

XIV.—MISCELLANEOUS.

In miscellaneous reading so much depends on individual taste, that no "short" nor "intermediate course" is given under the present head.

LIGHT SUBJECTS.

SPORT.—GAMES.

Herbert's (W. H.) ("Frank Forester") Field Sports; American Game in its Season; Fish and Fishing of the United States and Canada, etc.; Manual for Sportsmen.

Gerstaecker's (F.) Wild Sports of the West.

Napier's Wild Sports in Europe, Asia, and America.

Harris's Wild Sports of South Africa.

Gérard's Lion Hunting in Algeria.

Cumming's Five Years of a Hunter's Life in South Africa.

"Nimrod's" The Turf.

"Scrutator's" Practical Lessons in Hunting and Sporting. A most enjoyable book for all readers.

Shakespeare's (Captain H.) Wild Sports of India. Capital reading; both instructive and amusing.

Hamilton's (Col. J.) Reminiscences of an Old Sportsman. Abounds in "good stories capitally told," and in information of the greatest practical use to the sportsman.

Baker's (Sir S. W.) Rifle and Hound in Ceylon.

Norris's (T.) American Angler's Book.

† Walton's (Izaac) Complete Angler.

Scott's Fish and Fishing.

Carter's Summer Cruise.

Hardy's (Capt. C.) Forest Life in Acadie.

Hawker's Instructions to Young Sportsmen.

"Library of Wonders." Great Hunts.

Greenwood's (James) Wild Sports of the World.

Roosevelt's Game Fowl of the North.

Staunton's (H.) Chess Player's Hand-Book.

Fiske's Chess Tournament.

Sturgess's Guide to Draughts.

Cœlebs's Laws and Practice of Whist.

HUMOR AND SATIRE.

† Irving's (Washington) Knickerbocker's History of New York.

Irving and Paulding's Salmagundi.

Paulding's Diverting History of John Bull and Brother Jonathan.

† Hood (Thomas). Hood's Own; or, Laughter from Year to Year. 2 vols. 1st and 2d series with cuts.

Paulding's Three Wise Men of Gotham.

† Jerrold's (Douglas) Mrs. Caudle's Curtain Lectures; Story of a Feather; Punch's Letters to his Son; Wit and Humor of. Edited by Blanchard Jerrold.

† Thackeray's Yellowplush Papers; Shabby Genteel Story; Men's Wives; Book of Snobs; Fitz-Boodle's Confessions; Mr. Brown's Lectures to a Young Man about Town; Jeames's Diary; Paris Sketch-Book; Punch's Prize Novelist; History of Samuel Titmarsh; History of the Great Hoggarty Diamond; Christmas Books; Roundabout Papers.

Goethe's Reynard the Fox.

† Dickens's Pickwick Papers; Sketches by Boz.

Longstreet's Georgia Scenes.

Grimaldi's Shakespeare Notes.

"O'Dowd's (Cornelius)" Upon Men and Women, and other Things in General. From Blackwood.

† Smith (Sydney), Wit and Wisdom of. Edited by Duyckinck.

À Becket's Comic Blackstone; Comic History of England; Comic History of Rome.

Harte's (F. Bret) Condensed Novels, and other Papers. Comprising some admirable parodies, etc.

† Lowell's (J. R.) Biglow Papers.

Butler's (Sam.) Hudibras. A satire on the Puritans.

Combe's (W.) Dr. Syntax's Three Tours.

† Doran's Table Traits, with something on them.

† Maginn's Shakespeare Papers; Frazerian Papers; O'Doherty Papers.

De Mille's Dodge Club.

Burnand's Happy Thoughts. N. B. —See Father Prout; Horace Smith; the Ingoldsby Legends, under "Poetry."

Remark.—The Widow Bedott, Orpheus Kerr, Artemus Ward, Asa Hart's, etc., Papers, are popular with a certain class. Many condemn them as ephemeral in their character, and destitute of true humor. Some of the above writers carry their system of false spelling to an absurd and tiresome length.

ADVENTURES, TALES.

Falconer's (R.) Voyages, Adventures, and Imminent Escapes. In 1724. This is not the poet.

Martheilhe (Jean). The Huguenot Galley Slave.

Ellis's (Hon. G. A.) History of the State Prisoner, commonly called the "Iron Mask."

Watson's (H. C.) Nights in a Block House. Sketches of Border Life.

Captain Canot; or, Twenty Years of an African Slaver.

"Barry Cornwall's" Tales and Sketches.

Kincaid's (Captain) Adventures in the Rifle Brigade; Random Shots from a Rifleman.

Peters's (De Witt) Life and Adventures of Kit Carson.

Hilton's (Dav.) Brigandage in South Italy. A late and interesting account. [*See* also Moen's English Travellers and Italian Brigands.]

Davenport's Perilous Adventures.

Waters's (T.) Recollections of a Police Officer. By an inspector of the London Detective Corps.

Williams's (Dr. J. B.) Detective Stories.

† Stories from Blackwood.

THE MARVELLOUS AND CRIMINAL.

Scott's (Sir W.) Demonology and Witchcraft.

† Upham's Salem Witchcraft.

Denby's Philosophy of Mystery.

† Brewster's Natural Magic.

Ennemosor's History of Magic.

Williams (H.) The Superstitions of Witchcraft.

† Mackay's (Ch.) Memoirs of Extraordinary Popular Delusions. A most interesting production.

Mayo's Popular Superstitions.

Crowe's (Mrs.) Night-Side of Nature.

Holmes's (O. W.) Homœopathy and its Kindred Delusions.

Defoe's History of the Plague in London. 1665.

Feuerbach's German Criminal Trials.

Dumas's Celebrated Crimes.

Sargent's Planchette; or, the Despair of Science. A neat and interesting collection of facts and opinions about Spiritism.

LITERATURE, ART.

Walpole's Royal and Noble Authors.

† Disraeli's (I.) Curiosities of Literature. [*See* Belles-Lettres.]

Madden's Infirmities of Genius.

Bombaugh's (C. C.) Gleanings for the Curious.

"Milledulcia." Interesting Selections from Notes and Queries.

Burton (J. Hill). The Book-Hunter. Offers much amusement, as well as information.

Knight's (Ch.) Shadows of the Old Booksellers.

Spence's Anecdotes. A classic of its kind.

Bigelow's (L. J.) Bench and Bar.

Sedgwick's (T.) English Wigs and Gowns.

Jackson's (T.) Curiosities of the Pulpit.

Anonymous. Anecdotes of the American Clergy.

French's (Arbp.) Lessons on Proverbs.

Stearns's (Dr. C. N.) Shakespeare Treasury of Wisdom, etc.

Howitt's (Miss) Art Student in Munich.

Planche's New Literary Portraits.

Horne's New Spirit of the Age. Biographical Sketches.

Landor's (W. S.) Imaginary Conversations of Literary Men and Statesmen.

Doran's (Dr.) Annals of the Stage.

Vandenhoff's Leaves from an Actor's Note-Book.

Smith's (Sol.) Theatrical Management in the West and South for Thirty Years.

Morley (Prof.), Journal of a London Play-Goer.

HINTS ABOUT SPEAKING, WRITING, ETC.

Cornwallis's (Miss F. C.) Exposition of Vulgarisms, etc.

Gould's (E. G.) Good English correcting Popular Errors in Speaking and Writing.

Anonymous. Vulgarisms, and other Errors of Speech, including a chapter on Taste, and Examples of Bad Taste.

Taylor's (Rev. Isaac) Words and Places; or, Etymology Illustrative of History, Geography, etc.

Anonymous. Mistakes of Common Occurrence in Speaking and Writing.

† Peabody's (A. P.) Conversation: its Faults and Graces.

VARIOUS SUBJECTS.

† Irving's (Washington) Sketch-Book; Bracebridge Hall; Tales of a Traveller; Alhambra; Spanish Papers; Crayon Miscellany; Wolfert's Roost; "Book of the Hudson" (Rip Van Winkle, Sleepy Hollow).

† De Quincey's Confessions of an Opium-Eater; Narrative and Miscellaneous Papers; Letters to a Young Man; Note-Book of an English Opium-Eater; Avenger, and other papers.

† Willis's (N. P.) Pencillings by the Way; Letters from Under a Bridge; People I have Met; Health Trip to the Tropics, etc.

Doran's (Dr.) Knights and their

Days; Habits and Men; Monarchs Retired from Business.

Hunt (Leigh). Lord Byron and his Contemporaries; Legend of Florence; The Palfrey; Stories of the Italian Poets; Men, Women, and Books; Book for a Corner (selections in prose and verse). [*See* also "Poetry," "Essays," etc.]

Jameson's (Mrs.) Characteristics of Women; Diary of an Ennuyée; Legends of the Madonna; Legends of the Monastic Orders; Loves of the Poets; Studies and Stories. [*See* also Fine Arts.]

† Miller (Hugh). My Schools and Schoolmasters; First Impressions of England; Scenes and Legends of the North of Scotland; Tales and Sketches. [*See* also Travels, Geology, Essays.]

† Saunders's (Fred.) Salad for the Social; Salad for the Solitary; Mosaics; Festival of Song.

Blessington's (Countess of) Conversations with Lord Byron; Idler in Italy; Idler in France.

Anonymous. Homes of American Authors; Homes of American Statesmen.

Howitt's (W.) Homes and Haunts of Eminent British Poets (his most popular work); Visits to Remarkable Places; Old Halls, Battle-Fields, etc. (2d series.) Another interesting book, etc.

Dixon (Hep.) Her Majesty's Tower.

"Barry Gray's" Cakes and Ale at Woodbine; My Married Life at Hillside.

6

† Manning's (Miss) Household of Sir Thomas More (quite a little gem); Mary Powell.

Hall's (Mrs. S. C.) Sketches of Irish Character; Pilgrimages to English Shrines.

† Cooper's (Miss Fenimore) Rural Hours. A delightful series of country sketches.

† Wirt's (W.) Letters of a British Spy. An American classic.

† Longfellow's Outre Mer. Travelling sketches, in ease and grace, reminding us of Irving.

Davy's (Sir Humphry) Salmonia; or, Days of Fly Fishing; Consolations in Travel. Both excellent.

Bristed's Five Years in an English University.

Chasles's (Philarète) Studies from the German.

† Creasy's (Prof.) Fifteen Decisive Battles of the World.

Ottley's Remarkable Sieges, from Constantinople to Sevastopol.

Redding's (C.) Past Celebrities whom I have Known.

Lenox's (Lord W.) Drafts on my Memory.

Booth's (Rev. J., editor) Metrical Epitaphs, Ancient and Modern.

De Forest's (J.) European Acquaintances, etc.

Brown's (John) Sixty Years' Gleanings from Life's Harvest.

Martineau (Miss H.) Our Farm of Four Acres, etc.

† Michelet (Mme. J.) The Story of my Childhood. A fresh and exquisite picture of young French life.

† French's (W. S.) Realities of Irish Life. A notable book.

Hozier (Capt. H.) The British Expedition to Abyssinia.

† Mitchell's (D. G., "Ik Marvel") Dream Life; Wet Days at Edgewood.

† Everett's (Edward) Mount Vernon Papers.

More's (Sir Thomas) Utopia. Sketch of a model republic.

Bacon's (Lord) New Atlantis. A fancy picture like the last.

† Baring-Gould's Curious Myths of the Middle Ages. Curiosities of olden times.

Brinton's (D. G.) Myths of the New World.

† Wharton's (Grace and Philip) Queens of Society; Wits and Beaux of Society.

Knight's (Ch.) Half Hours with the Best Authors.

James's (Mrs.) Romance of Biography.

Liefde's (I. de) Romance of Charity.

Ildrewe's (Miss) Language of Flowers. Judicious.

Starling's (Miss) Noble Deeds of Woman.

† Brown's (Dr. John) Rab and his Friend; Marjorie Fleming. Two charming short sketches.

De Witt's (Madame—*née* Guizot) French Country Family.

Head's (Sir E.) Bubbles from the Brünnen of Nassau.

† Grattan's Highways and Byways.

Anonymous. Here and There; or, Notes of a Traveller.

Holbrook's (S. P.) Sketches by a Traveller.

Saunders's (F.) London, Literary and Historical.

† Heine's (H.) Pictures of Travel. Celebrated.

"The Colloquies of Edw. Osborne, Citizen and Clothworker." A quaint production.

Simmonds's Waste Products and Undeveloped Substances. Treats of beverages, food, perfumes, etc.

Head's (Sir E.) Stokers and Pokers. Under this whimsical title, contains excellent reading.

Brackenbury's (Captain) European Armaments in 1867.

McClellan's (Major-Gen.) Armies of Europe.

Tennent (Sir Emerson). The Story of Guns.

† Timbs's (John) Notable Things; Things not Generally Known.

Mann's (R.) Lessons in General Knowledge.

Craik's Pursuit of Knowledge under Difficulties, its Rewards and Pleasures.

Perry's (Miss) Five Hundred Employments adapted to Woman.

Simonin's (L.) Underground Life; or, Mines and Miners. Eminently interesting and instructive.

"Library of Wonders," embracing Meteors, Balloons, Optics, Heat, Electricity, etc., etc.

King's (C. W.) Natural History of Precious Stones, etc.

Emanuel on Gems.

Hazen's Popular Technology.

† Chambers's (Messrs.) Information for the People; Papers for the People; Pocket Miscellany, etc. All admirably adapted for entertainment and instruction.

Appletons' (Messrs.) Selections from the Quarterly Review. A choice literary banquet.

GRAVE SUBJECTS.

† Bacon's (Lord) Novum Organum; Advancement of Learning, etc. Bohn's edition, or condensed edition by Craik.

† Plato's Defence of Socrates; Phædo (on the immortality of the soul, and death of Socrates); The Republic, etc., etc. In Harper's "Classical Library."

† Burton's (R.) Anatomy of Melancholy. A delightful old classic.

† Browne's (Sir Thos.) Urn-Burial (Hydriotaphia). Another classic work. Some ancient sepulchral urns, which were dug up at Norfolk, England, formed the theme of this treatise, in which the author speculates on the vanity of human glory. Religio Medici (the religion of a physician). Full of quaint fancies.

Pascal's Thoughts. The beautiful production of a profound thinker. (From the French.)

Carlyle's (Thomas) Hero-Worship; † Sartor Resartus. Questions, philosophic, social, etc., discussed in a manner eminently original and thoughtful. An imaginary German professor serves as a lay figure. His most popular production.

† Oersted's Soul in Nature. A series of papers of exquisite beauty, on subjects philosophic, artistic, religious, æsthetic, etc., etc. Oersted was a Dane, of the very finest scientific eminence, and the discoverer of electro-magnetism.

† Emerson's (R. W.) Representative Men; Sermons and Orations. [*See* Essays.]

Hamilton's (Sir W.) Discussions on Philosophy and on Literature.

Gasparin's (Count) Science *versus* Modern Spiritualism.

† Draper (Dr. J. W.) A History of the Intellectual Development of Europe.

Darwin. On the Origin of Species by means of Natural Selection. [*See* Natural History.]

Lyell's (Sir Charles) Geological Evidences of the Antiquity of Man. [*See* Natural History.]

† Youmans (E. L.) The Culture demanded by Modern Life.

Milton (the poet). Treasures from the Prose Writings of. (Fields, Osgood & Co.)

† Landor (W. S.) Selections from the Writings of. By G. S. Hillard.

† Humboldt's (Alex. von) Cosmos; Aspects of Nature. Fascinating alike in style and subject.

† Taylor (Jeremy). Bishops Latimer, Barrow, etc., Selections from. By Basil Montagu. In weighty thought and poetic imagination equal to any thing in English literature.

Supplemental List.

† Hare's (A. & J.) Guesses at Truth. "Gems of Wisdom."

Mill (J. S.) The Subjection of Women.

Fuller's (Margaret) Woman in the Nineteenth Century.

Wotton's Reflections on Ancient and Modern Learning.

Eckermann's Conversations with Goethe.

Gladstone's (W. E.) Juventus Mundi; the Gods and Men of the Heroic Age.

Dupanloup's (Bishop) Studious Women. Advocates their higher culture. (From the French.)

Lankester's (Dr.) Lectures on the Uses of Animals to Man.

Cobbe's (Frances P.) Broken Lights. "An Inquiry into the Present Condition and Future Progress of Religious Faith." By a lady whose writings have lately won much attention.

Sale's Koran, etc. The sacred book of the Mahometans, containing the revelations which Mahomet pretended to have received from God.

Schoolcraft's Personal Memoirs of a Residence of Thirty Years with the Indian Tribes.

Bigelow's (Dr.) Nature in Disease.

Schaff's (Rev. Dr.) Germany: its Universities, Theology, etc.

† Richter (J. P.) Selections from. By Lady Chatterton.

* Sandford and Townsend's Great Governing Families of England.

Mallet's Northern Antiquities. (From the French.)

Keightley's Fairy Mythology.

Neligan's (Rev. W.) Rome: its Churches, Charities, and Schools. May be read with About's Roman Question.

Ruskin, the Beauties of. Selected by Mrs. L. C. Tuthill.

Colton's (Rev. C. C.) Lacon. A well-known collection of maxims, thoughts, etc.

† Argyle's (Duke of) Reign of Law (i. e., Law in a Scientific, or Metaphysical Sense). Much admired for its candor, manliness, and liberality of tone.

† Burke's (Peter) Wisdom and Genius of Edmund Burke. Selections in 1 vol., 8vo.

De Quincey, Beauties of.

Kingsley's Schools of Alexandria.

† Coleridge's (Sam'l T.) Biographia Literaria. Critical, philosophical, and literary memoranda and papers, with a biographical supplement.

XV.—PERIODICALS.

WITH a view to the requirements of libraries, the following list is made rather extensive.

REVIEWS.

American.	*British.*
North American (published in Boston).	Edinburgh (Whig).
Southern (published in Baltimore).	Quarterly (Conservative).
De Bow's (published in New Orleans).	Westminster (Liberal).
Church Review (New York).	North British (Free Church).
	Fortnightly (Liberal).
	Contemporary.

Remark.—The attention of all persons of literary taste is earnestly directed to the Reviews (and the best Magazines). They enable the man of little leisure to keep *au courant* with the world of thought—inform him of the new and valuable books brought out—give him, in a single article, the pith of most of them, and save him the trouble of reading the worthless. Messrs. Leonard Scott & Co., New York, republish the four first-named English Reviews and Blackwood.

MAGAZINES.

American.	*British.*
Atlantic Monthly (Boston).	Blackwood.
Appletons' Journal (New York).	Fraser's.
Harper's Monthly (New York).	Gentleman's.
Lippincott's Magazine (Philadelphia).	All the Year Round.
Eclectic (New York).	McMillan's.
New Eclectic (Baltimore).	Cornhill.
Galaxy (New York).	Cassell's.
Hunt's Magazine (New York).	Belgravia.
Our Young Folks (Boston).	Tinsley's.
Riverside (Boston).	London Society.
Good Words (reprint), (Philadelphia).	Temple Bar.
Good Words for the Young (reprint), (Philadelphia).	St. James's.
Sunday Magazine (reprint), (Philadelphia).	Victoria.
Overland Monthly (San Francisco).	St. Paul's.
Hours at Home (New York).	Chambers's Journal.
	Once a Week.
	Dublin University.
	Quiver.
	Bow Bells.
	Notes and Queries.

APPENDIX.

I.—BOOKS OF REFERENCE.

DICTIONARIES.

English.—Webster's, or Worcester's, or Chambers's, or Donald's, Etymological Dictionaries.

French.—Spiers and Surenne's, or Surenne's.

German.—Adler's, or Elwell's (small 8vo). Hilpert's, or Flügel's; both large.

Spanish.—Velasquez.

Italian.—Meadows's, 16mo, or Milhouse's, 2 vols., 8vo.

Latin.—Andrews's, or Anthon's, or Leverett's.

Greek.—Liddell and Scott's. Edited by Drisler.

Remark.—Many other valuable dictionaries are published besides the above. Of most of the large ones, abridgments can be had.

ENCYCLOPÆDIAS.

Appletons' New American Cyclopædia. 16 large vols. For the American reader this is by far the best published. Every year, beginning with 1861, an annual volume has been published, bringing the work down to the present day.

Chambers's Cyclopædia. 10 large vols. An excellent work.

Remark.—For public libraries, etc., there are many other cyclopædias still larger. Of these, the Encyclopædia Britannica, in 22 vols., may be specified.

ATLASES.

Colton's, or Black's, or Mitchell's, etc., etc. Many of these are ancient as well as modern. An ancient atlas is indispensable to a student. Long's Ancient Atlas; Gage's Historical Atlas, exhibiting the varying names and boundaries in the map of Europe for centuries back—much-needed, cheap and handy publication.

MISCELLANEOUS.

Literature.—Duyckinck's Cyclopædia of American Literature. 2 vols., large 8vo. Brought down to 1865. Chambers's Cyclopædia of English Literature. 2 vols., large 8vo. Allibone's Dictionary of English Literature. 3 vols., large 8vo. Dr. Smith's Classical Dictionary. Dr. Smith's Dictionary of Greek and Roman Antiquities. Roget's Thesaurus of English Words and Phrases. Poole's Index to Periodical Literature. Graham's English Synonymes. Or, Wedgwood's, or Crabbe's.

Religion.—Cruden's Concordance of the Old and New Testament. Horne's Introduction to the Study of the Holy Scriptures. Of commentaries, Henry's, Scott's, Lange's, Barnes's, and Cowles's, may be enumerated. Dr. Smith's Comprehensive Bible Dictionary. 3 vols. in 1 vol., large 8vo. Edited by Dr. Barnum; with maps, cuts, etc. Admirably adapted to popular need. McClintock and Strong's Bible Cyclopædia. 3 vols., 8vo. Kitto's Cyclopædia of Biblical Knowledge. 3 vols., 8vo.

Medicine.—Dunglison's Medical Dictionary, or Copland's. 3 large vols.

Law.—Bouvier's Law Dictionary.

Farming.—Johnson's Farmer's and Planter's Encyclopædia. 1 vol., large 8vo.

Science and Arts.—Appletons' Dictionary of Mechanics, Engineering, etc. Ure's Dictionary of Arts, Manufactures, etc. Brande's Cyclopædia of Science, Literature, and Art. Edition of 1867. Nichols's Cyclopædia of the Physical Sciences. Maunder's Treasury of Science and Literature. 1 vol., 18mo.

Commerce.—McCulloch's Commercial Dictionary. Edition of 1869 by his son. De Veitelle's Mercantile Dictionary of Commercial Terms in English, Spanish, and French.

Philosophy.—Fleming's Vocabulary of Philosophy. Edition of C. P. Rauth, D. D.

Geology.—Page's Hand-Book of Geological Terms.

Geography.—Lippincott's Pronouncing Gazetteer. 1 vol., large 8vo. Or, McCulloch's Geographical Dictionary. Edition by Martin, 1866. Beeton's Dictionary of Geography. 1 vol., small 8vo.

Biography.—Appletons' Cyclopædia of Biography. Cyclopædia of Biography, by Parke Godwin. Hole's Brief Biographical Dictionary. Martin's Brief Dictionary of Contemporary Biography. * "Men of the Times." A small 8vo volume published annually. Lippincott's Dictionary of Biography and Mythology. To those acquainted with German or French, the works of * Dr. Hoeffer, and the * "Biographie Universelle," 85 vols., can be confidently recommended.

History.—Sir H. Nicolas's Chronicle of History. Frank Moore's Rebellion Record.

Chronology.—Putnam's World's Progress. Latest edition. Haydn's Dictionary of Dates. Two American reprints. Or, Blair's or Tegg's Chronology.

Bibliography.—* Lowndes's Bibliographer's Manual. 4 vols., 8vo. * Dibdin's Library Companion. Jewett's Public Libraries in the United States. 1 vol., 8vo. * Edwards's Memoirs of Libraries. 2 vols., 8vo. * Brunet's Manual. 5 vols., 8vo. In French. The best in existence, but out of print.

Various.—Wheeler's Noted Names of Fiction. Highly useful, and the only publication of the kind. Mary Cowden Clarke's Concordance of Shakespeare. Bartlett's Familiar Quotations. Fifth edition. Dictionary of Latin Quotations. Includes Mottoes, Law Terms, etc., etc., with translations, etc. Bartlett's Americanisms. Third edition. Bohn's Cyclopædia of Political, Statistical, etc., Knowledge. Haldeman's Affixes to English Words. Beckmann's History of Inventions, etc. 4 vols., 8vo. Matthias's Rules of Order, etc.; or, Manual for conducting Business in Public Meetings. Harper's Cyclopædia of Household Science. Maunder's Treasury of Botany. 2 vols., 8vo. Maunder's Treasury of Knowledge, and Library of Reference. 1 vol., 18mo. Appletons' Iconographic Cyclopædia. 6 vols. Illustrated with 500 steel engravings. Cyclopædia of Commercial and Business Anecdotes. 2 vols., 8vo. Burton's Cyclopædia of Wit and Humor. 2 vols., 8vo.

Remark.—Besides the above-named works, cyclopædias or dictionaries of music, the drama, architecture, and, indeed, of most branches of knowledge, have been published.

II.—BOOKS FOR PARENTS AND HOUSEKEEPERS.

FOR PARENTS.

Combe's (Dr. Andrew) Management of Infancy, Physiological and Moral. Best edition by Sir J. Clarke, 1860. This work has maintained a high reputation for nearly half a century. Or,

Chavasse's (Dr.) Advice to Mothers on the Management of their Offspring. Seventh edition. Or,

Getchell's (Dr. F. H.) Maternal Management of Infancy.

Nightingale's (Florence) Notes on Nursing, etc. Judicious and Practical.

Beecher's (Catharine E.) Training of Children. Should be *studied* by every mother.

FOR HOUSEKEEPERS.

Blot's (Prof.) What to Eat, and How to Cook it. Hand-Book of Practical Cookery.

Warren's (Mrs.) How to Furnish a Dwelling-House on Small Means.

Maling's (Miss E.) Indoor Plants, and How to Rear Them. Of practical value, and displaying good taste.

Supplemental List.

Youmans's (E. L.) Household Science.

Haskins's What to Eat. An account of the most common adulterations of food and drink.

Putnam's (publisher) What Shall we Eat?

Bellows's Philosophy of Eating.

Breakfast, Dinner, and Tea.

Soyer's Domestic Cookery.

Six Hundred Dollars a Year.

Hints on Household Taste in Furniture and Upholstery, etc.

Haskell's (Mrs.) Housekeeper's Cyclopædia of Useful Information. Embracing cookery, canning, preserving, domestic economy, etc., etc.

Field's (M.) Green-Houses and Green-House Plants.

Wright's Book of 3,000 Useful Receipts. Compiled with care and excellent judgment.

Cooley's Book of Useful Knowledge. Containing 6,000 practical receipts, etc.

III.—BOOKS FOR THE YOUNG.

There are few things in the field of authorship demanding more taste and judgment, it might almost be said genius, than to write appropriate books for the young. It follows, as a necessary consequence, that there exists no little difficulty in *selecting* appropriate books of this class. Accordingly, I undertake an office so responsible with much diffidence. I venture to do so, however, from the necessity of the case, and invariably supported by good authority. It may be seen from the list below that I have a predilection for the old-fashioned boys' classics, fairy tales, works of imagination, and such as *insensibly* foster truth, manliness, and gentleness. Nor do I care to conceal a hearty disgust for much of the teeming literature of the day prepared for the young. Fortunately, there are exceptions, and these not a few; many living authors of distinction do not disdain writing for youthful as well as adult readers.

BOOKS FOR THE YOUNG—Entertaining.

Defoe's Robinson Crusoe.

Wyss's (D. von) Swiss Family Robinson.

Forster's (translator) Arabian Nights. Boy's edition.

Cottin's (Madame) Elizabeth; or, the Exiles of Siberia.

Swift's (Dean) Gulliver's Travels. Boy's edition.

Edgeworth's (Miss) Tales. 10 vols. "Helen" is generally regarded as the best.

Johnson's (Dr. S.) Rasselas, Prince of Abyssinia.

Aikin's, etc., Evenings at Home.

Lamb's (Miss) Stories from Shakespeare.

Grimm's Household Stories. Home Stories.

Marryat's (Captain) Masterman Ready. Children of the New Forest. Settlers in Canada. Scenes in Africa. Stories of the Sea, etc.

Hawthorne's Wonder Book for Boys and Girls. Tanglewood Tales.

Paulding's Gift from Fairy Land.

Clarke's (Mrs. Cowden) Many Happy Returns of the Day. A capital "Boy's Own Book."

Howitt's (W.) A Boy's Adventures in Australia.

Morley's (Prof.) Fairy Tales.

Scott's (M.) Tom Cringle's Log.

Aulnoy's (Countess d') Fairy Tales.

Lea & Blanchard's (publishers) Boys' Treasury of Sports.

Labourdaye's Fairy Tales.

Reid's (Capt. Mayne) Desert Home. Forest Exiles. Boy Hunters. Young Voyageurs. Bush Boys. Young Yägers. Plant Hunters. Ran Away to Sea. The Boy Tar. Odd People. Bruin. Cliff Climbers. Ocean Waifs. Afloat in the Forest. Boy Slaves. Giraffe Hunters. An admirable writer for the young.

Follen's (Eliza L.) Home Dramas for Young People. Compiled chiefly from Bertram, Edgeworth, etc.

McIntosh's (Miss) Aunt Kitty's Tales.

Osborne's (Capt.) Quedah. Just the book for a boy.

"Anonymous." The Water Babies, a Fairy Tale, etc. "A more delightful book was never written to refresh the wearied brain."

Sherwood's (Mrs.) Tales. 15 vols. In the cases of such voluminous writers as Mrs. Sherwood, Miss Edgeworth, and Charlotte Elizabeth, a selection is suggested.

Conscience's (H.) Tales. A Belgian writer.

Macé's (Jean) Home Fairy Tales. From the French.

Hall's (Mrs. S. C.) Uncle Sam's Money-Box.

"Holme Lee's" Fairy Tales.

Day's Sandford and Merton.

"Grace Greenwood's" Stories from Famous Ballads. History of my Pets. Recollections of my Childhood, etc.

"Peter Parley's" Tales of Adventure. Story of La Perouse. Popular Natural History. Consisting mainly of anecdotes, etc.

Du Chaillu's Wild Life under the Equator. Stories of the Gorilla Country. Lost in the Jungle.

Baker's (Sir S. W.) Cast Up by the Sea. Rifle and Hound in Ceylon. Sir S. is a favorite with Boys.

Ingelow's (Jean) Mopsa the Fairy. Exquisite.

St. Pierre's (Bernardin) Paul and Virginia.

Andersen's (Hans C.) Tales and Fairy Stories.

Mulock's (Miss) Fairy Tales for Children.

Martineau's (Harriet) Settlers at Home. Peasant-Boy and the Prince. Feats on the Fiord. The Crofton Boys.

Greenwood's (James) Wild Sports of the Traveller.

Frere's Old Deccan Days.

Cooper's (J. F.) Leather-Stocking Tales.

Bowman's (Anne) Kangaroo Hunters. Young Exiles, etc.

Ballantyne's Deep Down. Erling the Bold. Fighting the Flames.

Carroll's (Lewis) Alice's Adventures in Wonder Land.

Aldrich's (Th. B.) Story of a Bad Boy.

Anonymous. The Sociable; or, 1,001 Amusements.

" Amateur Theatricals.

" How to Amuse an Evening Party.

Frost's Book of Tableaux.

BOOKS FOR THE YOUNG—Instructive.

"I am sure children and the lower classes of readers hate books which are written *down* to their capacity, and prefer those which are written for their elders."—*Sir Walter Scott.*

Mayhew's Young Benjamin Franklin.

" Peasant-Boy Philosopher. Wonders of Science.

Wood's (Rev. G.) Homes without Hands. Describing the homes of animals.

Hooker's Child's Book of Nature.

Bulfinch's (T.) Stories of Gods and Heroes. Or,

Cox's (G. W.) Tales of Ancient Greece. Includes the author's Tales of Mythology, Tales of Gods and Heroes, Tales of Thebes, etc.

Goulding's (F. B.) Young Marooner.

Dalton's (W.) The English Boy in Japan.

"Actæa's" First Lessons in Natural History. Men who Have Risen.

Schnorr, Overbeck's, etc., Bible Picture-Book.

"Young American's Library." 9 vols. A very judicious selection, including Hudson, Capt. J Smith, Daniel Boone, etc., etc.

Abbott's Illustrated Biographies. 30 vols. Comprising Alexander the Great, Julius Cæsar, Hannibal, Alfred, Mary Queen of Scots, Henry IV., Peter the Great, Cortez, etc.

Heydenreich's (Rev. L.) Life of Gustavus Adolphus.

"Peter Parley's" Anecdotes of the Animal Kingdom. Wonders of Geology. Lives of Benefactors.

Edgar's (John G.) Boyhood of Great Men. Footprints of Famous Men. Sea-Kings, etc.

Schnorr's Outlines. Pictorial.

Simms's (W. G.) Life of Capt. John Smith. Life of Gen. Francis Marion.

Hooker's First Book in Chemistry. First Book in Natural History.

Dickens's (Charles) Child's History of England.

Wood's Illustrated Natural History.

"Oliver Bunce's" Romance of the Revolution.

Davenport's Perilous Adventures. Inculcate lessons of courage, perseverance, and patience.

Scott's (Sir Walter) Tales of a Grandfather. Narrating the history of Scotland.

Duyckinck's (George) Lives of George Herbert, Bishops Ken, Latimer, and Jeremy Taylor.

Plutarch's Lives. 1 vol. Abridged edition.

Russell's (W.) Boyhood, etc., of Extraordinary Men.

Frost's (John) Book of the Indians. Border Wars of the West. Wild Scenes of a Hunter's Life.

"Library of Wonders." Embracing:

- The Meteors. With 25 Wood Engravings.
- Balloons. By Camille Flammarion. 20 Illustrations.
- The Great Hunts. By Victor Mennier.
- Railways. Illustrated with 111 Vignettes.
- The Wonders of Architecture. By André.
- The Wonders of Naval Art.
- Celestial Wonders. By C. Flammarion.
- Parks and Gardens. 26 Vignettes.
- The Metamorphoses of Insects. 30 Vignettes.
- The Wonders of the Vegetable World.
- The Wonders of Optics.
- Volcanoes and Earthquakes.
- Grottoes and Caverns.
- Heat. Illustrated with 90 Cuts.
- The Wonders of Electricity.

"Oliver Optic's" Young America Abroad. The Lake Shore Series, etc.

IV.—A FEW HINTS TO THOSE INTENDING TO ENTER BUSINESS, OR ANY OF THE PROFESSIONS OR TRADES.

PROFESSIONS, BUSINESS, Etc.

For the benefit of young persons intending to prosecute some profession or business, etc., and who wish to turn to use spare time *before* commencing their regular training, I give below the titles of a few books suitable for this purpose. I say a *few*, for it is worth recollecting that *one good text-book thoroughly mastered* is of more profit than *half a dozen read hurriedly or negligently.* But, although the advantages of preparatory reading are undoubted, it is in the counting-room, the hospital, the lawyer's office, etc., where knowledge of practical importance is chiefly gathered. I should premise that the hints are specially intended for youths not residing in large cities.

TEACHING.

The profession of teaching is, in some degree, an exception to the remarks just made; for, the more varied a teacher's information, the more profound and completely at his command, the better prepared will he be to perform the duties of his profession. And this information is, in a good measure, what is called "book-knowledge." The arts of communicating this knowledge, and of school-government, in themselves of such vast importance to the teacher, are, it would seem, innate; but something may be learned from the experience of others; the truth of this conclusion normal schools have proved beyond question. To young teachers without special training, and desirous to learn something about the various theories afloat respecting modes of instruction, discipline, school-curricula, and the many other educational questions now agitated, the following works are suggested; the list might be extended a hundred-fold:

Locke's (John) Essay on Education.

Mann's (Horace) Educational Reports. The seventh treats of Education in Europe.

Barnard's (Prof. H.) Educational Reports, etc.

Potter and Emerson's Manual for Teachers. (See similar works by Abbott and Prof. Hart, etc.)

Youmans's (Dr. E. L.) Culture demanded by Modern Life. Advocates the claims of science.

Lives of T. Arnold, Pestalozzi, etc.

Hope's (Ascott R.) A Book about Boys. A Book about Dominies. Genial and sensible.

Thompson's (D'Arcy) Wayside Thoughts.

Cousin's (Victor) Report on Education in Prussia. Education as *projected*, not legislated upon, *in full.*

Arnold's (Matthew) Schools, etc., on the Continent.

Carlyle's, Froude's, Lowe's, and Mill's Addresses. 1 vol. Arnold's book and the Addresses are interesting and valuable.

Spencer's (Herbert) Education, Intellectual, Moral, and Physical. By one of the profoundest thinkers of the day.

MEDICINE.

My advice to a youth intending "to study medicine," and having some spare time *before* entering a medical college, would be to confine his attention to one or two of the branches of a medical curriculum; let us say physiology and anatomy. As to text-books, commence with an *elementary* work on physiology; Youmans and Huxley's, or Draper's, for instance. As soon as you have acquired a *thorough knowledge* of this elementary work, write to the dean or president of the college which you intend entering, and get the titles of the prescribed text-books for the two branches named above; confine your studies (previous to entering college) to these. The use of two or more text-books on one subject for a beginner—except for consultation—is highly injudicious. If you cannot decide upon a college, you will be safe in selecting Carpenter or Müller for physiology, and Wilson for anatomy. Get the latest editions. As subsidiary studies, I would advise to keep up your Latin and Greek; if unacquainted with German, by all means commence it, as it is practically of the greatest use to the physician. For light reading, the Lives of Hunter, Boerhaave, Abernethy, Sir Henry Halford, etc., are suggested.

LAW.

To the law-student (*in prospectu*) ambitious of honorable distinction, much of the counsel given in the last chapter but one is equally applicable. Whether at the bar or in the senate, the illustrations to be drawn from history, the poets, or literature generally, lend force and point even to the ablest argument. Frequently, also, cases come before the courts involving questions in the mechanical arts, in chemistry, mercantile usages, etc. It is true the lawyer can "read up" for these occasions; but, to do this speedily and effectively, previous general acquaintance with the subject is evidently of the greatest value. Nor should the law-student neglect legal biography: here he will find these desultory remarks borne out by the greatest examples; he will see eminent lawyers devoting leisure hours to the pursuits of elegant literature, to physical science, or mathematics. I take for granted an acquaintance with at least Latin and one or more modern languages; so, I shall now merely add the titles of a few books which will give the student a general view into his intended profession. I name only one text-book, to be read *decies repetitus.*

Anthon's Law Student. 1 vol., 8vo. Or,

Hoffman's (David) Course of Legal Study.

Warren's Introduction to Law Studies. The 12mo edition.

* Smith's (P. A.) History of Education for the English Bar. The last two works, though English publications, would no doubt prove valuable on this side of the Atlantic. Also * Moseley's Hand-Book.

Lives of Chief-Justice Marshall, the Livingstones (Robert and Edward), Wirt, Story, Kent, Webster, Flanders's "Lives of the Chief Justices," and Lord Campbell's "Lives."

Blackstone's Commentaries.

MERCANTILE LIFE.

The experience of others, as contained in books, and the training of the intellect by study, are not valuable to the lawyer and doctor alone; every man, no matter what his occupation, and no matter what his own skill or knowledge, it may be safely said, has something to learn from his fellow-man. The merchant, the farmer, the dyer, the brewer, etc., can always pick up some new idea from the written experience of his co-laborer. Books, journals, magazines, giving information upon all branches of business, constitute a fair portion of our present stock of literature. Below I give merely titles of works treating generally of their respective subjects; works of a special character can be had of the bookseller, or ordered through him. In the large cities the public libraries generally furnish a sufficient supply. It is almost needless to add that general mental culture offers the same pleasures and benefits to the mechanic as to any other man, and should be appreciated by him accordingly.

Hunt's (Freeman) Collection of Maxims, etc.

Hillard's (G. S.) Dangers and Duties of the Mercantile Profession.

Munroe & Co.'s (publishers) Readings for Young Men, etc.

"The Successful Merchant." S. Budgett.

"The Successfnl Merchant." W. Arthur.

Hunt's (Freeman) Lives of American Merchants.

Anderson's Practical Mercantile Letter-Writer.

De Veitelle's Mercantile Dictionary. In three languages.
Bourne's Famous London Merchants. 1 vol., 16mo.
Anonymous. Importance of Literature to Men of Business.

FARMING.

Stöckhardt's (Dr. J. A.) Chemical Field Lectures.
Johnston's (J. F. W.) Catechism of Agricultural Chemistry and Geology. Has attained a thirty-third edition.
Johnston's (J. F. W.) Lectures on Agricultural Chemistry, etc. This is a larger work.
Mitchell's (D. G.) Rural Studies. Wet Days at Edgewood.
Downing's (A. J.) Architecture of Country Houses.
Morris's (Edmund) Ten Acres Enough. How to Get a Farm, and Where to Find One.
Roosevelt's Five Acres Too Much.
Haraszthy's Grape Culture, Wines, and Wine-making.

MECHANICAL OCCUPATIONS.

Bakewell's Great Facts. A popular history of remarkable inventions during the present century.
Howe's Lives of Eminent Mechanics.
Foucaud's Lives of Illustrious Mechanics.
Smiles's Industrial Biography. Lives of George and Robert Stephenson Workmen's Earnings. Strikes and Savings.
Report of English Mechanics concerning the Paris Exposition.
Timb's Inventors and Discoverers.
Wrigley's (Edmund) Workingman's Way to Wealth; a Practical Treatise on Building Associations, etc.

V.—ADDITIONAL WORKS FOR A LIBRARY.

Under the above head I have given the titles of some additional books which, from their voluminousness, the nature of the subjects treated, or, for other reasons, were deemed unsuitable for the preceding classified lists; also, the collected works of some distinguished men, authors and others.

No attempt has been made here, or in the body of this work, to give *prices;* these vary so much with different editions, and from the present fluctuating value of gold. Two dollars and a half per volume may be taken as a fair *average.*

Authors, all of whose works have been cited elsewhere, are, with few exceptions, omitted here. Full sets of the American and British poets are indispensable to a good library. Many of those named in the following lists have written extensively in prose:

Complete Works of

Adams (John).
Addison.[1]
Arnold (Thomas).
Bacon.[2]
Bentham.
Bolingbroke.
Browne (Sir T.)
Browning (Mrs.)
Browning (Robt.)
Bryant.
Burke.[3]
Burns.
Butler (Bishop).
Calhoun.
Chalmers (Thos.)
Channing.
Chaucer.
Clay.
Coleridge.
Cooper (J. F.)
Cowper.
Defoe.
De Quincey.
Disraeli (Is.)[4]
Dryden.[5]
Edwards (Jona).
Emerson.
Epictetus.[6]
Everett (Alex. H.)
Fielding.
Franklin.
Goethe.[7]
Goldsmith.
Guizot.
Hall (Robt.)
Hamilton (Alex.)
Hamilton (Sir W.)
Hazlitt.
Heeren.
Hobbes.[8]
Hume.
Irving (W.)
Jefferson.
Johnson (S.)
Jonson.
Lamb.[9]
Longfellow.
Lowell.
Macaulay.
Madison.
Milton.
Moore.
Montaigne.
Pope.
Plato.
Prescott.
Raleigh.
Richter.[10]
Ruskin.
Schiller.
Scott.
Shakespeare.
Smollett.
Southey.
Spencer (H.)
Spenser.
Sterne.
Swift.
Taylor (Jer.)
Tennyson.
Washington.
Webster.
Whittier.
Wordsworth.

---

[1] Edition by Prof. Greene.
[2] Edition by Heath and Spedding.
[3] Edition of Little, Brown & Co., Boston.
[4] Edition by Sir G. C. Lewis.
[5] Edition by Sir W. Scott.
[6] Edition (English) by T. W. Higginson.
[7] Edition published by Bohn, London.
[8] Edition by Sir W. Molesworth.
[9] Edition by Talfourd.
[10] Edition (English) by Prof. Evans.

N. B.—The editions of foreign authors are generally limited to their most celebrated productions.

HISTORY—some Additional Works.

United States.

Pickett's History of Alabama.
Forbes's, or Capron's, California.
Williamson's North Carolina.
Ramsay's, or Simms's, South Carolina.
Dwight's, or Trumbull's, Connecticut.
Irving's (Theodore) Florida.
Arthur's, or Stephens's, Georgia.
Belknap's New Hampshire.
Gordon's, or Mulford's, New Jersey.
Butler's, or Arthur's, Kentucky.
Gayarre's Louisiana.
Williamson's Maine.
McSherry's Maryland.
Barry's, or Minot's, Massachusetts.
Lanman's Michigan.
Neil's, or Bond's, Minnesota.
Flint's Mississippi Valley.

Gordon's, or Proud's, Pennsylvania.
Arnold's Rhode Island.
Ramsay's Tennessee.
Maillard's, or Yoakum's, Texas.
Ferris's Utah.
Williams's Vermont.
Harrison's, or Campbell's, Virginia.
Ritchie's Wisconsin.
Palfrey's New England.
Dunlap's, or Smith's, New York.
Flint's Western States.
O'Callaghan's New Netherlands.

N. B.—Many of the above are out of print.

British America.

Martin's History of the Canadas.
Bonnycastle's Newfoundland in 1842.
Martin's Nova Scotia.

Europe.

Burnet's (Bishop) History of his Own Times; History of the Reformation.
Clarendon's (Lord) History of the Great Rebellion.
Schlosser's History of the Eighteenth Century.
Vertot's Revolutions of Spain and Portugal.
Paul's (Father) History of the Council of Trent.
Cunningham's (Rev. J.) Church History of Scotland. Accurate, impartial, and vivacious in style.
Ranke's History of Servia. In same volume is included Cyprien Robert's Slave Provinces of Turkey.

BIOGRAPHY—some Additional Works.

Stone's Life of Sir W. Johnston (1715–'74). 2 vols.
Sparks's Life of Gouverneur Morris.
Sedgwick's Life of W. Livingston.
Kapp's Life of F. W. von Steuben.
Wheaton's Life of W. Pinkney.
Tudor's Life of Otis.
Johnston's Life of Gen. Greene.
Dale's (S.) Life of Gen. Claiborne.
Raymond's Life of Pres't Lincoln. Or by Holland.
Holland's (Lady) Life of Sydney Smith.
Coxe's Lives of Sir Robert and Horace Walpole.
Life of Sir Robert Peel. By trustees of his papers.
Guizot's Life of Sir Robert Peel. Treats incidentally of the Pritchard indemnity, Tahiti Protectorate, etc.
Tulloch's (Rev. Dr. J.) Leaders of the Reformation. Attractive in style and liberal in treatment.
Russell's (Earl) Life and Times of Lord W. Russell.
Life of T. Hood. By his Daughter.
Butler's Lives of the Saints.
Rémusat's (Charles de) Bacon, sa Vie, son Temps, etc. (In French.) Able and impartial.
Life of Sir James Mackintosh. By his Son.
Life of F. Perthes. By his Son. Perthes was a distinguished bookseller, etc., of Hamburg and Gotha.
Medwin's Life of Shelley.

Bourne's (H. R.) Memoirs of Sir Philip Sidney.

Biddle's Memoir of Cabot.

Espinasse's Life of Voltaire. Highly recommended.

Trollope's (T.) Decade of Italian Women.

Carlyle's Life of John Sterling. Excellent.

Life of Horner. By his Brother.

Brooks's (C. T.) Life of Jean Paul F. Richter.

Jerrold's (Blanchard) Life of Douglas Jerrold.

Twiss's (H.) Public and Private Life of Lord Eldon.

Barrow's (Sir J.) Lives of Howe and Anson.

TRAVELS AND VOYAGES.

Ruxton's Mexico, and the Rocky Mountains.

Bartlett's Explorations in Texas, New Mexico, etc.

Baxley's West Coast of South and North America.

Herndon's, etc., Valley of the Amazon. 3 vols.

Wise's (Lieut. H. A.) Los Gringos. (Mexico and California.)

Strain's (J. G.) Chili and the Argentine Provinces.

Ruxton's Life in the Far West.

Palmer's (Dr. J. W.) Sketches in California and India.

Wilde's (W. R.) Voyage to Madeira, Teneriffe, etc., etc.

Anonymous. Madeira, Portugal, and the Andalusias.

Bickmore's East-Indian Archipelago. 8vo.

Rushenberger's Voyage round the World (1835–'37).

PHILOSOPHY, LOGIC, THEOLOGY—some Additional Works.

Warburton's (Bishop) Divine Legation of Moses. Reply to Lord Bolingbroke.

Kurtz (Dr.) The Bible and Astronomy. Against Deism and Pantheism.

Stewart's (Dugald) Collected Works. Edition of Sir W. Hamilton.

Newman's (J. H.) Apologia pro Vitâ Suâ. An eloquent vindication of his religious course.

Supplemental List.

Strauss's Life of Jesus. Edition of 1864. This is a new and popular life, with a modified application of his peculiar views.

Schleiermacher's Lectures on the Life of Christ. Holds a position between Strauss and the orthodox. As a pious, conscientious man, Schleiermacher was universally respected.

Renan's Life of Jesus.

Ewald's Life of Jesus. Written to controvert the views of Strauss and Renan.

Pressense's Jesus Christ, His Life, Times, and Work. French orthodox view. Ably written.

Hase's (Rev. Dr. Carl) Life of Jesus. Rewritten in 1860, to meet Strauss's myth theory.

Wesley's (John) Life of Christ.

Beecher's Life of Christ.

Powell (Rev. Baden). The Order of Nature considered in reference to the Claims of Revelation. This furnishes an able and impartial résumé of the various rationalistic and naturalistic theories on biblical miracles. Reviews also Paulus, Strauss, and Ewald, etc.

Kant's Critique of Pure Reason. A celebrated metaphysical work.

"Essays and Reviews." By Profs. Powell, Williams, Temple, etc. The most desirable edition is that of 1865, with the important passages marked.

"Aids to Faith." By Mansel, Rawlinson, etc., etc. A series of able theological papers, in reply to the "Essays and Reviews."

"Replies to Essays and Reviews." By several clergymen, with preface by the present Bishop of Winchester.

Hooker's Laws of Ecclesiastical Polity. A defence of the ministry and ceremonies of the Anglican Church.

Shipley (Rev. Orby, editor). The Church and the World. 3 vols. An exposition of the views and objects of the Ritualists. Is heartily abused and praised.

Maurice (Rev. F. D.) Theological Essays. These, and the other writings of Maurice, are marked by eminent purity and catholicity of spirit.

Newman's (Prof. F. W.) Phases of Faith; or, Passages from the History of my Creed. The sixth edition, with the answer to Prof. Rogers's "Eclipse of Faith," is the best.

Spinoza's Critical Inquiry into the Hebrew Scriptures. "Will be welcomed in its new [alluding to the translation into English] dress by all liberal students. An introduction and notes add to its value."—*W. Review*, 1863.

Bunsen's (Baron) God in History; or, the Progress of Man's Faith in the Moral Order of the World.

Beard (J. R., editor). The Progress of Religious Thought, as illustrated in the Protestant Church of France, etc. A series of Essays and Reviews, by Scherer, of Geneva; Colani, of Strasbourg; Reville, at Rotterdam; Schotten, of Leyden; Renan, of Paris, etc.

White's Emanuel Swedenborg, his Life and Writings.

Wilkinson's Life of Swedenborg.

Edwards's (Jonathan) Inquiry, etc., into the Freedom of the Will. World-renowned as a piece of exact reasoning.

Moehler's (J. A.) Symbolism; or, the Doctrinal Differences between Catholics and Protestants as represented by their Public Confessions of Faith. A truly remarkble book; was first published in 1832.

Döllinger's (J. J.) Heathenism and Judaism, the Vestibule of the History of Christianity. A masterly survey of the religious and moral condition of the world at the advent of Christ.

POLITICAL ECONOMY, LAW, POLITICS—some Additional Works.

Livingston's System of Penal Laws. A law classic.

Boeckh's Public Economy of Athens.

Benton's Thirty Years in the United States Senate. Abridgment of the Debates in the United States Congress.

Works of "Peter Porcupine." By W. Cobbett. Indispensable to the student of early American politics.

Brougham's (Lord) Colonial Policy of the European Powers.

"The Madison Papers."

Phillimore's Commentaries on International Law. Valuable and interesting to historical readers, as well as to lawyers.

Cobden's (Richard) Political Works.

Beck's Medical Jurisprudence.

NATURAL HISTORY AND NATURAL PHILOSOPHY.

Cuvier's Natural History. Translated by Griffith and others.

Schoolcraft's Ethnological Researches respecting the Red Men of America.

Vogt's (Dr. Carl) Lectures on Man: his Place in Creation and in the History of the Earth. Is a fierce enemy to orthodoxy in science, as well as in religion and politics.

Unger's Botanical Letters.

Schacht's On the Microscope. The last two are popular works.

Remark.—For more complete information on any special point in natural history, the large work of Sir W. Jardine (in forty volumes) may be consulted; also, Cuvier (edition above-named). Cuvier is one of the greatest, if not the greatest name, in this department of science. Buffon, and his translator (as he may be called), Goldsmith, although delightful writers, are deficient in accuracy.

POETRY, ESSAYS, MEMOIRS, LETTERS, Etc.

Humboldt's (Alex. von) Letters to Varnhagen von Ense. This correspondence, extending over a period of thirty years (1827–'58), has made some curious revelations.

Guizot's Memoirs to illustrate the History of My Own Times.

Rabelais's Complete Works. Edited by Bohn. With notes and commentaries. (From the French.)

Sterne's (Laurence) Sentimental Journey. Tristram Shandy.

Shaftesbury's (Lord) Characteristics.

St. Augustine's Confessions. Edited by W. Shedd.

Brown's (Sir Thomas) Vulgar Errors.

Fielding's Amelia. Joseph Andrews. Tom Jones.

Bourke's (Sir B.) Vicissitudes of Families, and other Essays. Displays in a striking manner the instability of human greatness.

Swinburne's Atalanta in Calydon. Song of Italy. Poems.

Boccaccio's Decameron.

Foster's (John) Contributions to the Eclectic Review. Sir J. Mackintosh pronounced Foster to be one of the ablest and most original of English thinkers.

Garrick's Correspondence. Edited by Sir Joshua Reynolds.

Cicero's (first century before Christ) Offices. Tusculan Disputations. Essays on Friendship and Old Age. (Harper's Classical Library.)

Marlowe, Ben Jonson, Massinger, Beaumont and Fletcher, Ford, Webster, Otway, Rowe, etc., portions of. These are some of the early British dramatists. Charles Lamb edited an admirable volume of selections. The most noted of the later dramatists are mentioned under the head Poetry. Mrs. Inchbald edited with considerable taste a collection, entitled British Theatre, in twenty-five small volumes.

Heine's (H.) Lutèce. (From the German.) "These letters upon the social, artistic, and political life of France, are full of wit, and show an astonishing prescience in their famous author."—*North American Review*, 1856.

Blanco White's Memoirs.

VI.—MODERN LANGUAGES.

In a work like the present—aiming to shape the literary culture of young persons who may consult it—a few remarks about the study of modern languages will, perhaps, not be deemed inappropriate.

It is unnecessary, I fancy, to dwell upon the *practical* importance to many of this kind of study. We have all heard of the saying of Charles V., "The man who knows two languages has two lives and two souls." To the traveller, to most persons in business, to those expecting to be engaged in literary pursuits, or in journalism, some acquaintance with modern tongues is wellnigh indispensable. Even to the man who reads for mental cultivation, or merely for amusement, this kind of knowledge is most valuable. We can never thoroughly appreciate the work of a foreign author except in its original form; the subtle essence of the book escapes us in the translation, no matter how excellent it may be, just as we miss the *bouquet* of a fine wine in the adulterated mixture, however skilfully concocted.

Fortunately, the apparatus for acquiring foreign languages are now good and ample, suited to all ages and different tastes. Especially is this the case as regards text-books for learning to speak and write German, French, etc. Thanks to Herr Ollendorff, we have got rid of the absurdities of phrase-books and the prolixities of Manesca. Philosophy and common-sense are enlisted in favor of the "natural system."

Before proceeding to give a list of some text-books, I would say to those whose chief object in this matter is to learn how *to speak*—who are without an instructor, and with but little time at command—not to expect nor to aim at much progress in a short time; with patience and perseverance, success is sure. Short lessons, of say five to fifteen minutes, frequently repeated, will be found the most efficacious. At the outset the aid of a teacher to get the correct pronunciation is very desirable. It is a common observation that children learn to speak foreign languages quicker than adults, and servants than their employers. Among other reasons which readily account for this, may be mentioned the *limited vocabulary* in use with children and servants, and the *constant repetition* of their small stock of words and phrases. This lesson should not be lost on the learner; the study of the grammar (as far as the inflections are concerned) should *all along* be carefully kept up. Opinions differ, it is proper to state, on this point.

With respect to matter for translation, choose something idiomatic, and likely to be of use in the vocabulary of words taught; for instance, a good play, or the "items" column of a newspaper. Select the simplest possible translation at first.

If in a foreign country, the student will find it advantageous to visit frequently the theatre, law courts, churches, etc. To understand the spoken language is at first much harder than to speak it.

TEXT-BOOKS—Modern Languages.

Marcel's (C.) The Study of Languages brought back to its True Principles. 1 vol., 12mo. Highly recommended for its sensible and original views.

Prendergast's (Th.) Mastery Series. This is a new method, so far applied only to German, French, and Hebrew; it dispenses with the use of grammar, and, for *adults* able to devote only a few minutes to study at occasional and uncertain intervals, it offers undoubted advantages. The "Mastery" method has been tried in Europe with great success.

Andrews's New French Instructor. 1 vol., 12mo.

Ollendorff's New Method of Learning French. 1 vol. Also, for German, Spanish, and Italian.

Ahn's French Method. 1 vol., 12mo. Also for German and Spanish. This series is smaller and more elementary than the last.

De Vere's Grammar in French. 1 vol., 12mo. Similar in general plan to Ollendorff.

Remark.—There are also similar works to the above by Fasquelle (French), Woodbury (German), Otto (German). They are all supplied with keys for the use of students without an instructor.

De Fivas's Elementary French Reader. Classical French Reader. Both very judicious in selections.

Collot's Dramatic French Reader. Gives some of the best French dramas entire.

De Vere's First French Reader. Edited with excellent taste and judgment.

Adler's German Reader. A model work of the kind. The selections admirably made in all respects, and the notes just what are needed.

Velasquez's Spanish Reader. 1 vol., 12mo.

Foresti's Italian Reader. 1 vol., 12mo.

Remark.—The above are given as specimens. Many other valuable works of the kind are published.

VII.—ASSUMED OR CHANGED NAMES.

By "changed" names are meant those changed by marriage, or the assumption of a title. Many assumed names—of authors insignificant whether for worth or wit—have been intentionally omitted. It is feared that some names in the list below fall under the category, but the writers referred to have attained a certain notoriety, so it was thought better to gratify those curious in such trifles. Where the name is evidently fictitious, it is cited in the same order of words as written, or, as it is usually called by:

"Alfred Crowquill"—A. H. Forester.

"A. L. O. E." (a lady of England)—Miss Charlotte Tucker.

"An Old Boy"—Thomas Hughes ("Tom Brown").

"Arthur Sketchley"—George Rose.

"Artemus Ward"—Charles F. Browne.

"Asa Trenchard"—H. Waterson.
"Austin (Miss Lucy)"—Lady Duff Gordon.
"A Veteran Observer"—E. D. Mansfield.
"Bard (Samuel A.)"—Ephraim G. Squier.
"Barrett (Walter)"—Joseph A. Scoville.
"Barry Cornwall"—B. W. Procter.
"Barry Gray"—R. B. Coffin.
Beecher (Miss H.)—Mrs. H. B. Stowe.
"Bee Hunter"—Colonel T. B. Thorpe.
"Benauly"—Benjamin Austin and Lyman Abbott, jointly.
"Berger (E.)"—Miss Eliza Sheppard.
"Bill Arp"—Charles H. Smith.
"Blythe White, Jr."—Solon Robinson.
"Bon Gaultier"—Thomas Martin.
Bronté (Anne)—"Acton Bell."
" (Charlotte)—"Currer Bell" (Mrs. Nicholls)
" (Emily)—"Ellis Bell."
Bulwer (Edward L.)—Lord Lytton (created baronet in 1835).
"Burleigh"—Matthew H. Smith.
Burney (Fanny)—Madame D'Arblay.
"Carl Benson"—Charles Astor Bristed.
"Caroline Fry"—Mrs. Wilson.
"Cecil Davenant"—Rev. D. Coleridge.
"Charlotte Elizabeth"—Mrs. C. E. Tonna.
"Christopher North"—Professor Wilson.
"Country Parson"—Rev. A. H. Boyd.
"Cousin Alice"—Alice B. Haven.
Craik (Mrs.)—Miss Mulock.
"Creyton (Paul)"—J. T. Trowbridge.
"Cuthbert Bede"—Rev. E. Bradley.
"Daisy Howard"—Myra Daisy McCrum.
D'Arblay (Madame)—Fanny Burney.
"Delta" (of *Blackwood*)—D. W. Moir.
"Dick Tinto"—J. C. Goodrich.
"Doesticks (Q. K. Philander)"—Mortimer Thompson.
"Dr. Oldham, of Greystones"—Caleb S. Henry, LL. D.
"Downing (Major Jack)"—Seba Smith.
"Dun Browne"—Rev. Samuel Fiske.
"Elia"—Charles Lamb.
"Eliot (George)"—Miss Evans; now Mrs. Lewes.

"Ettrick Shepherd (The)"—James Hogg.
Evans (Miss Augusta)—Mrs. Wilson.
"Fanny Fern"—Mrs. Parton, *née* Willis.
"Fat Contributor"—A. M. Griswold.
"Father Prout"—Mahoney.
"Figaro"—H. Clapp, Jr.
"Fleta"—Kate W. Hamilton.
"Florence Percy"—Mrs. Eliza Akers.
"Frank Forester"—W. H. Herbert.
Fuller (Margaret)—Countess d'Ossoli.
"Gail Hamilton"—Miss Abigail Dodge.
"Georges Sand"—Madame Dudevant, *née* Dupin.
"Grace Greenwood"—Mrs. Lippincott.
"Harry Franco"—C. F. Briggs.
"Harry Gringos"—A. H. Wise, U. S. N.
"Harland (Marion)"—Mrs. M. V. Terhune.
"Helen Mar"—Mrs. D. M. F. Walker.
"Historicus"—W. G. Vernon-Harcourt.
"Holme Lee"—Miss Parr.
"Ik Marvell"—D. G. Mitchell.
"Irenæus" (New York *Observer*)—Rev. I. S. Prime.
"January Searle"—George S. Phillip.
"Jeems Pipes"—Stephen C. Massett.
"Jennie June"—Mrs. Jennie Croly.
"John Phenix"—Capt. G. H. Derby, U. S. A.
"Josh Billings"—H. W. Shaw.
"Kirke (Edmund)"—J. R. Gilmore.
"Laurie Todd"—Grant Thorburn.
"Lounger" (*Harper's Magazine*)—G. W. Curtis.
"McArone"—George Arnold.
"Mace Sloper"—C. G. Leland.
"Malakoff" (New York "*Times*")—Dr. Johnson.
"Mary Clavers (Mrs.)"—Mrs. C. M. Kirkland.
"Miles O'Reilly"—Col. Charles G. Halpine.
"Minnie Myrtle"—Miss Anne L. Johnson.
Morpeth (Lord)—Earl of Carlisle.
Mowatt (Mrs.)—Mrs. Ritchie, *née* Ogden.
Mulock (Miss)—Mrs. Craik.
"Ned Buntline"—E. Z. C. Judson.
"Nimrod" ("*Bell's Life*")—Charles J. Apperly.

"Novalis"—F. von Hardenberg.
"Oliver Optic"—W. T. Adams.
"Orpheus C. Kerr (i. e., *office-seeker*)—R. H. Newell.
Ossoli (Countess d')—Margaret Fuller.
"Ouida"—Miss La Ramé.
"Owen Meredith"—Robert Bulwer Lytton.
"Partington (Mrs.)"—B. P. Shillaber.
"Pepper (K. N., *cayenne pepper*)"—J. W. Morris.
"Perley" (also "Raconteur")—Major Ben Perley Poore.
"Peter Parley"—S. Griswold Goodrich.
"Peter Pindar"—Dr. John Wolcot.
"Petroleum V. Nasby"—Dr. Locke (*editor of Toledo Blade*).
Piozzi (Madame)—Mrs. Thrale, *née* Salisbury.
"Porte Crayon"—Gen. D. H. Strother.
Prescott (Miss Harriet)—Mrs. R. G. Spofford.
"Pylodet (L., an anagram)—E. Leypoldt.
"Regester Seely"—Mrs. O. J. Victor.
"Shirley Dare"—Miss Susan Dunning.
"Syntax (Dr.)"—W. Combe.
"Talvi" (*anagram*)—Mrs. Prof. E. Robinson, *née* T. A. L. von Jacob.
"Timothy Titcomb"—Dr. J. G. Holland.
"Thomas (Miss Annie)"—Mrs. Pender Cudlip.
"Tom Brown" ("An Old Boy")—Thomas Hughes, M. P.
"Trafford (F. G.)"—Mrs. J. H. Riddell.
"Trusta" (*anagram*)—Mrs. E. Stuart Phelps.
"Wetherell (The Misses)"—The Misses Warner.
Wilson (Mrs.)—Miss Augusta Evans.

VIII.—A FEW ANONYMOUS WORKS, WITH NAMES OF AUTHORS, REAL OR IMPUTED.

Ecce Homo. By Professor Seely (?).
Ecce Cœlum. By Rev. E. F. Barr.
Phases of Faith. By Prof. F. W. Newman.
Eclipse of Faith. By Prof. H. Rogers.
Nemesis of Faith. By J. A. Froude.
Essays and Reviews. By Profs. Powell, Williams, Temple, etc.
New Gospel of Peace. By Richard Grant White.
Schönberg-Cotta Family Series. By Mrs. E. Charles.
Mary Powell. By Miss Manning.

Household of Sir Thomas More. By Miss Manning.
Rural Hours. By Miss S. Fenimore Cooper.
Lyrics by the Letter H. By Col. C. G. Halpine.
Spirit of '76. By Mrs. D. S. Curtis.
Lacon. By Rev. C. C. Colton.
Home, Sweet Home (song). By J. Howard Payne.
Marseillaise (words and air). By Rouget de Lisle.
Partant pour la Syrie. By Queen Hortense.
Sparrow-Grass Papers. By F. S. Cozzens.
Porcupine Papers. By W. Cobbett, etc.
Provincial Letters. By Blaise Pascal.
Drapier's " " Dean Swift.
Chinese " " Oliver Goldsmith.
Junius's " " Sir Philip Francis (?).
Inchiquin " " C. J. Ingersoll.
Peter Plymley's Letters. By Sydney Smith.
Paul's Letters to his Kinsfolk. By Sir Walter Scott.
Peter's " " " " J. G. Lockhart.
Greyson Letters. By Prof. H. Rogers.
Swiss Family Robinson. D. von Wyss.
Rutledge. By Miss Miriam Cole (now Mrs. Harris).
Beulah. By Miss Augusta Evans.
The Lamplighter. By Miss M. S. Cummings.
Erring yet Noble. By Isaac F. Reed.
Faith Gartney's Childhood. By Mrs. A. D. T. Whitney.
Tales of the Genii. By Rev. James Ridley.
Guy Livingstone. By J. Lawrence.
Mademoiselle Mori. By Charles Clarke.

THE END.

LIST OF WORKS

PUBLISHED BY D. APPLETON & CO.,

90, 92 & 94 GRAND ST., NEW YORK.

A Descriptive Catalogue, with full titles and prices, may be had gratuitously on application.

About's Roman Question.
Adams' Boys at Home.
—— Edgar Clifton.
Addison's Spectator. 6 vols.
Adler's German and English Dictionary.
—— Abridged do. do. do.
—— German Reader.
—— " Literature.
—— Ollendorff for Learning German.
—— Key to the Exercises.
—— Iphigenia in Tauris.
After Icebergs with a Painter.
Agnel's Book of Chess.
Aguilar's Home Influence.
—— Mother's Recompense.
—— Days of Bruce. 2 vols.
—— Home Scenes.
—— Woman's Friendship.
—— Women of Israel. 2 vols.
—— Vale of Cedars.
Ahn's French Method.
—— Spanish Grammar.
—— A Key to same.
—— German Method. 1 vol.
Or, separately—First Course. 1 vol.
Second " 1 vol.
Aids to Faith. A series of Essays, by Various Writers.
Aikin's British Poets. From Chaucer to the Present Time. 3 vols.
Album for Postage Stamps.
Albums of Foreign Galleries; in 7 folios.
Alden's Elements of Intellectual Philosophy.
Alison's Miscellaneous Essays.
Allen's Mechanics of Nature.
Alsop's Charms of Fancy.
Amelia's Poems.
American Poets (Gems from the).
American Eloquence. A Collection of Speeches and Addresses. 2 vols.
American System of Education:
1. Hand-Book of Anglo-Saxon Root-Words.
2. Hand-Book of Anglo-Saxon Derivatives.

American System of Education:
3. Hand-Book of Engrafted Words.
Anderson's Mercantile Correspondence.
Andrews' New French Instructor.
—— A Key to the above.
Annals of San Francisco.
Antisell on Coal Oils.
Anthon's Law Student.
Appletons' New American Cyclopædia of Useful Knowledge. 16 vols.
—— Annual Cyclopædia, and Register of Important Events for 1861, '62, '63, '64, '65.
—— Cyclopædia of Biography, Foreign and American.
—— Cyclopædia of Drawing.
The same in parts:
Topographical Drawing.
Perspective and Geometrical Drawing.
Shading and Shadows.
Drawing Instruments and their Uses.
Architectural Drawing and Design.
Mechanical Drawing and Design.
—— Dictionary of Mechanics and Engineering. 2 large vols.
—— Railway Guide.
—— American Illustrated Guide Book. 1 vol.
Do. do., separately:
1. Eastern and Middle States, and British Provinces. 1 vol.
2. Southern and Western States, and the Territories. 1 vol.
—— Companion Hand-Book of Travel.
Arabian Nights' Entertainments.
Arnold's (S. G.) History of the State of Rhode Island. 2 vols.
Arnold's (Dr.) History of Rome.
—— Modern History.
Arnold's Classical Series:
—— First Latin Book.
—— First and Second Latin Book and Grammar.
—— Latin Prose Composition.
—— Cornelius Nepos.
—— First Greek Book.
—— Greek Prose Composition Book, 1.

Arnold's Greek Prose Composition Book, 2.
—— Greek Reading Book.
Arthur's (T. S.) Tired of Housekeeping.
Arthur's (W.) Successful Merchant.
At Anchor; or, A Story of our Civil War.
Atlantic Library. 7 vols. in case.
Attaché in Madrid.
Aunt Fanny's Story Book.
—— Mitten Series. 6 vols. in case.
—— Night Cap Series. 6 vols. in case.

Badois' English Grammar for Frenchmen.
—— A Key to the above.
Baine's Manual of Composition and Rhetoric.
Bakewell's Great Facts
Baldwin's Flush Times.
—— Party Leaders.
Balmanno's Pen and Pencil.
Bank Law of the United States.
Barrett's Beauty for Ashes.
Bartlett's U. S. Explorations. 2 vols.
—— Cheap edition. 2 vols. in 1.
Barwell's Good in Every Thing.
Bassnett's Theory of Storms.
Baxley's West Coast of America and Hawaiian Islands.
Beach's Pelayo. An Epic.
Beall (John Y.), Trial of.
Beauties of Sacred Literature.
Beauties of Sacred Poetry.
Beaumont and Fletcher's Works. 2 vols.
Belem's Spanish Phrase Book.
Bello's Spanish Grammar (in Spanish).
Benedict's Run Through Europe.
Benton on the Dred Scott Case.
—— Thirty Years' View. 2 vols.
—— Debates of Congress. 16 vols.
Bertha Percy. By Margaret Field. 12mo.
Bertram's Harvest of the Sea. Economic and Natural History of Fishes.
Bessie and Jessie's Second Book.
Beza's Novum Testamentum.
Bibles in all styles of bindings and various prices.
Bible Stories, in Bible Language.
Black's General Atlas of the World.
Bloomfield's Farmer's Boy.
Blot's What to Eat, and How to Cook it.
Blue and Gold Poets. 6 vols. in case.
Boise's Greek Exercises.
—— First Three Books of Xenophon's Anabasis.
Bojesen's Greek and Roman Antiquities.
Book of Common Prayer. Various prices.
Boone's Life and Adventures.
Bourne's Catechism of the Steam Engine.
—— Hand-Book of the Steam Engine.
—— Treatise on the Steam Engine.
Boy's Book of Modern Travel.
—— Own Toy Maker
Bradford's Peter the Great.
Bradley's (Mary E.) Douglass Farm.
Bradley's (Chas.) Sermons.
Brady's Christmas Dream.
Breakfast, Dinner, and Tea.
British Poets. From Chaucer to the Present Time. 8 large vols.
British Poets. Cabinet Edition. 15 vols.
Brooks' Ballads and Translations.
Brown, Jones, and Robinson's Tour.
Bryan's English Grammar for Germans.
Bryant & Stratton's Commercial Law.
Bryant's Poems, Illustrated.
—— Poems. 2 vols.
—— Thirty Poems.
—— Poems. Blue and Gold.
—— Letters from Spain.
Buchanan's Administration.
Buckle's Civilization in England. 2 vols.
—— Essays.
Bunyan's Divine Emblems.
Burdett's Chances and Changes.
—— Never Too Late.
Burgess' Photograph Manual. 12mo.
Burnett (James R.) on the Thirty-nine Articles.
Burnett (Peter H.), The Path which led a Protestant Lawyer to the Catholic Church.
Burnouf's Gramatica Latina.
Burns' (Jabez) Cyclopædia of Sermons.
Burns' (Robert) Poems.
Burton's Cyclopædia of Wit and Humor. 2 vols.
Butler's Martin Van Buren.
Butler's (F.) Spanish Teacher.
Butler's (S.) Hudibras.
Butler's (T. B.) Guide to the Weather.
Butler's (Wm. Allen) Two Millions.
Byron Gallery. The Gallery of Byron Beauties.
—— Poetical Works.
—— Life and Letters.
—— Works. Illustrated.

Cœleb's Laws and Practice of Whist.
Cæsar's Commentaries.
Caird's Prairie Farming.
Calhoun's Works and Speeches. 6 vols.
Campbell's (Thos.) Gertrude of Wyoming.
—— Poems.
Campbell (Judge) on Shakespeare.
Canot, Life of Captain.
Carlyle's (Thomas) Essays.
Carreno's Manual of Politeness.

Carreno's Compendio del Manual de Urbanidad.
Casseday's Poetic Lacon.
Cavendish's Laws of Whist.
Cervantes' Don Quixote, in Spanish.
—— Don Quixote, in English.
César L'Histoire de Jules. par S. M. I. Napoleon III. Vol. I., with Maps and Portrait. (French.)
Cheap Edition, without Maps and Portrait.
Maps and Portrait, for cheap edition, in envelopes.
Champlin's English Grammar.
—— Greek Grammar.
Chase on the Constitution and Canons.
Chaucer's Poems.
Chevalier on Gold.
Children's Holidays.
Child's First History.
Choquet's French Composition.
—— French Conversation.
Cicero de Officiis.
Chittenden's Report of the Peace Convention.
—— Select Orations.
Clarke's (D. S.) Scripture Promises.
Clarke's (Mrs. Cowden) Iron Cousin.
Clark's (H. J.) Mind in Nature.
Cleaveland and Backus' Villas and Cottages.
Cleveland's (H. W. S.) Hints to Riflemen.
Cloud Crystals. A Snow Flake Album.
Cobb's (J. B.) Miscellanies.
Coe's Spanish Drawing Cards. 10 parts.
Coe's Drawing Cards. 10 parts.
Colenso on the Pentateuch. 2 vols.
—— On the Romans.
Coleridge's Poems.
Collins' Amoor.
Collins' (T. W.) Humanics.
Collet's Dramatic French Reader.
Comings' Physiology.
—— Companion to Physiology.
Comment on Parle a Paris.
Congreve's Comedy.
Continental Library. 6 vols. in case.
Cooke's Life of Stonewall Jackson.
Cookery, by an American Lady.
Cooley's Cyclopædia of Receipts.
Cooper's Mount Vernon.
Copley's Early Friendship.
—— Poplar Grove.
Cornell's First Steps in Geography.
—— Primary Geography.
—— Intermediate Geography.
—— Grammar School Geography.
—— High School Geography and Atlas.
—— High School Geography.
—— " " Atlas.
—— Map Drawing. 12 maps in case.
—— Outline Maps, with Key. 13 maps in portfolio.
—— Or, the Key, separately.
Cornwall on Music.
Correlation and Conservation of Forces.
Cortez' Life and Adventures.
Cotter on the Mass and Rubrics.
Cottin's Elizabeth; or, the Exiles of Siberia.
Cousin Alice's Juveniles.
Cousin Carrie's Sun Rays.
—— Keep a Good Heart.
Cousin's Modern Philosophy. 2 vols.
—— On the True and Beautiful.
—— Only Romance.
Coutan's French Poetry.
Covell's English Grammar.
Cowles' Exchange Tables.
Cowper's Homer's Iliad.
—— Poems.
Cox's Eight Years in Congress, from 1857 to 1865.
Coxe's Christian Ballads.
Creasy on the English Constitution.
Crisis (The).
Crosby's (A.) Geometry.
Crosby's (H.) Œdipus Tyrannus.
Crosby's (W. H.) Quintus Curtius Rufus.
Crowe's Linny Lockwood.
Curry's Volunteer Book.
Cust's Invalid's Book.
Cyclopædia of Commercial and Business Anecdotes. 2 vols.

D'Abrantes' Memoires of Napoleon. 2 vols.
Dairyman's (The) Daughter.
Dana's Household Poetry.
Darwin's Origin of Species.
Dante's Poems.
Dasent's Tales from the Norse.
Davenport's Christian Unity and its Recovery.
Dawson's Archaia.
De Belem's Spanish Phrase-Book.
De Fivas' Elementary French Reader.
—— Classic French Reader.
De Foe's Robinson Crusoe.
De Girardin's Marguerite.
—— Stories of an Old Maid.
De Hart on Courts Martial.
De L'Ardeche's History of Napoleon.
De Peyrac's Comment on Parle.
De Staël's Corinne, ou L'Italie.
De Veitelle's Mercantile Dictionary.
De Vere's Spanish Grammar.
Dew's Historical Digest.
Dickens's (Charles) Works. Original Illustrations. 24 vols.
Dies Irae and Stabat Mater, bound together.
Dies Irae, alone, and Stabat Mater, alone.
Dix's (John A.) Winter in Madeira.
—— Speeches and Addresses. 2 vols.

Dix's (Rev. M.) Lost Unity of the Christian World.
Dr. Oldham at Greystones, and his Talk there.
Doane's Works. 4 vols.
Downing's Rural Architecture.
Dryden's Poems.
Dunlap's Spirit History of Man.
Dusseldorf Gallery, Gems from the.
Dwight on the Study of Art.
Ebony Idol (The).
Ede's Management of Steel.
Edith Vaughan's Victory.
Egloffstein's Geology and Physical Geography of Mexico.
Eichhorn's German Grammar.
Elliot's Fine Work on Birds. 7 parts, or in 1 vol.
Ellsworth's Text-Book of Penmanship.
Ely's Journal.
Enfield's Indian Corn; its Value, Culture, and Uses.
Estvan's War Pictures.
Evans' History of the Shakers.
Evelyn's Life of Mrs. Godolphin.
Everett's Mount Vernon Papers.

Fables, Original and Selected.
Farrar's History of Free Thought.
Faustus.
Fay's Poems.
Fénélon's Telemaque.
——— The same, in 2 vols.
——— Telemachus.
Field's Bertha Percy.
Field's (M.) City Architecture.
Figuier's World before the Deluge.
Fireside Library. 8 vols. in case.
First Thoughts.
•Fiji and the Fijians.
Flint's Physiology of Man.
Florian's William Tell.
Flower Pictures.
Fontana's Italian Grammar.
Foote's Africa and the American Flag.
Foresti's Italian Extracts.
Four Gospels (The).
Franklin's Man's Cry and God's Gracious Answer.
Frieze's Tenth and Twelfth Books of Quintilian.
Fullerton's (Lady G.) Too Strange Not to be True.
Funny Story Book.

Garland's Life of Randolph.
Gaskell's Life of Brontë. 2 vols.
The same, cheaper edition, in 1 vol.
George Ready.
Gerard's French Readings.
Gertrude's Philip Randolph.
Gesenius' Hebrew Grammar.
Ghostly Colloquies.
Gibbes' Documentary History. 3 vols.
Gibbons' Banks of New York.
Gilfillan's Literary Portraits.
Gillespie on Land Surveying.
Girardin on Dramatic Literature.
Goadby's Text-Book of Physiology.
Goethe's Iphigenia in Tauris.
Goldsmith's Essays.
——— Vicar of Wakefield.
Gosse's Evenings with the Microscope.
Goulburn's Office of the Holy Communion.
——— Idle Word.
——— Manual of Confirmation.
——— Sermons.
——— Study of the Holy Scriptures.
——— Thoughts on Personal Religion.
Gould's (E. S.) Comedy.
Gould's (W. M.) Zephyrs.
Graham's English Synonymes.
Grandmamma Easy's Toy Books.
Grandmother's Library. 6 vols. in case.
Grand's Spanish Arithmetic.
Grant's Report on the Armies of the United States 1864-'65.
Grauet's Portuguese Grammar.
Grayson's Theory of Christianity.
Greek Testament.
Greene's (F. H.) Primary Botany.
—— Class-Book of Botany.
Greene's (G. W.) Companion to Ollendorff.
—— First Lessons in French.
—— First Lessons in Italian.
—— Middle Ages.
Gregory's Mathematics.
Griffin on the Gospel.
Griffith's Poems.
Griswold's Republican Court.
——— Sacred Poets.
Guizot's (Madame) Tales.
Guizot's (M.) Civilization in Europe. 4 vols.
—— School edition. 1 vol.
—— New Edition, on tinted paper. 4 vols.
Gurowski's America and Europe.
——— Russia as it is.

Hadley's Greek Grammar.
Hahn's Greek Testament.
Hall's (B. H.) Eastern Vermont.
Hall's (C. H.) Notes on the Gospels. 2 vols.
Hall's (E. H.) Guide to the Great West.
Halleck's Poems.
—— Poems. Pocket size, blue and gold.
—— Young America.
Halleck's (H. W.) Military Science.
Hamilton's (Sir Wm.) Philosophy.
Hamilton's (A.) Writings. 6 vols.

Hand-Books on Education.
Hand-Book of Anglo-Saxon Root-Words.
Hand-Book of Anglo-Saxon Derivatives.
Hand-Book of the Engrafted Words.
Handy-Book of Property Law.
Happy Child's Library. 18 vols. in case.
Harkness' First Greek Book.
—— Latin Grammar.
—— First Latin Book.
—— Second "
—— Latin Reader.
Hase's History of the Church.
Haskell's Housekeeper's Encyclopædia.
Hassard's Life of Archbishop Hughes.
—— Wreath of Beauty.
Haupt on Bridge Construction.
Haven's Where There's a Will There's a Way.
—— Patient Waiting no Loss.
—— Nothing Venture Nothing Have.
—— Out of Debt Out of Danger.
—— Contentment Better than Wealth
—— No Such Word as Fail.
—— All's Not Gold that Glitters.
—— A Place for Everything, and Everything in its Place.
—— Loss and Gain.
—— Pet Bird.
—— Home Series of Juvenile Books. 8 vols. in case.
Haven (Memoir of Alice B.).
Hazard on the Will.
Hecker's Questions of the Soul.
Hemans' Poems. 2 vols.
—— Songs of the Affections.
Henck's Field-Book for Engineers.
Henry on Human Progress.
Herbert's Poems.
Here and There.
Herodotus, by Johnson (in Greek).
Herodotus, by Rawlinson (in English). 4 vols.
Heydenreich's German Reader.
Hickok's Rational Cosmology.
—— Rational Psychology.
History of the Rebellion, Military and Naval. Illustrated.
Hoffman's Poems.
Holcombe's Leading Cases.
—— Law of Dr. and Cr.
—— Letters in Literature.
Holly's Country Seats.
Holmes' (M. A.) Tempest and Sunshine.
—— English Orphans.
Holmes' (A.) Parties and Principles.
Homes of American Authors.
Homer's Iliad.
Hooker's Complete Works. 2 vols.
Hoppin's Notes.
Horace, edited by Lincoln.
Howitt's Child's Verse-Book.
—— Juvenile Tales. 14 vols. in case.
How's Historical Shakspearian Reader.
—— Shakspearian Reader.
Huc's Tartary and China.
Hudson's Life and Adventures.
Humboldt's Letters.
Hunt's (C. H.) Life of Livingston.
Hunt's (F. W.) Historical Atlas.
Huntington's Lady Alice.
Hutton's Mathematics.
Huxley's Man's Place in Nature.
—— Origin of Species.

Iconographic Encyclopædia. 6 vols.—4 Text and 2 Plates.
Or, separately:
The Countries and Cities of the World. 2 vols.
The Navigation of all Ages. 2 vols.
The Art of Building in Ancient and Modern Times. 2 vols.
The Religions of Ancient and Modern Times. 2 vols.
The Fine Arts Illustrated. 2 vols.
Technology Illustrated. 2 vols.
Internal Revenue Law.
Iredell's Life. 2 vols.
Italian Comedies.

Jacobs' Learning to Spell.
—— The same, in two parts.
Jaeger's Class-Book of Zoology.
James' (J. A.) Young Man.
James' (H.) Logic of Creation.
James' (G. P. R.) Adrien.
Jameson's (Mrs.) Art Works.
—— Legends of Saints and Martyrs. 2 vols.
—— Legends of the Monastic Orders.
—— Legends of the Madonna.
—— History of Our Lord. 2 vols.
Jarvis' Reply to Milner.
Jay on American Agriculture.
Jeffers on Gunnery.
Jeffrey's (F.) Essays.
Johnson's Meaning of Words.
Johnson's (Samuel) Rasselas.
Johnston's Chemistry of Common Life. 2 vols.

Kavanagh's Adele.
—— Beatrice.
—— Daisy Burns.
—— Grace Lee.
—— Madeleine.
—— Nathalie.
—— Rachel Gray.
—— Seven Years.
—— Queen Mab.
—— Women of Christianity.
Keats' Poems.

Keep a Good Heart.
Keightley's Mythology.
Keil's Fairy Stories.
Keith (Memoir of Caroline P.)
Kendrick's Greek Ollendorff.
Kenny's Manual of Chess.
Kinglake's Crimean War. Vols. 1 and 2.
Kirke White's Poems.
Kirkland's Life of Washington.
A Cheaper Edition, for Schools.
Knowles' Orlean Lamar.
Kœppen's Middle Ages.
—— Separately—Middle Ages, 2 vols.
——— Atlas.
Kohlrausch's History of Germany.
Kuhner's Greek Grammar.

Lafever's Beauties of Architecture.
Lady Alice.
Lamartine's Confidential Disclosures.
——— History of Turkey. 3 vols.
Lancelott's Queens of England, and their Times. 2 vols.
Landon's (L. E.) Complete Works.
Latham's English Language.
Layard's Nineveh. Illustrated.
—— Cheap edition. Without Illustrations.
Learning to Spell.
Le Brun's Telemaque.
Lecky's Rise and Influence of Rationalism. 2 vols.
Le Sage's Adventures of Gil Blas. 1 vol.
—— Gil Blas, in Spanish.
Letter Writer.
Letters from Rome.
Lewes' (G. H.) History of Philosophy. 2 vols.
—— In 1 vol.
—— Physiology of Common Life.
Library of Travel and Adventure. 3 vols. in case.
Library for my Young Countrymen. 9 vols. in case.
Libro Primario de Ortografia.
Liebig's Laws of Husbandry.
Life of Man Symbolized by the Months of the Year.
Light and Darkness
Lights and Shadows of New York Picture Galleries.
Lindsay's Poems.
Linn's Life and Services.
Little Builder.
Little Engineer.
Livy, with English Notes.
Logan's Château Frissac.
Looking Glass for the Mind.
Lord's Poems.
—— Christ in Hades: a Poem.
Louise.
Lunt's Origin of the Late War.
Lyell's Elements of Geology.
Lyell's Principles of Geology.
Lyra Americana.
Lyra Anglicana.

Macaulay's Essays. 1 vol.
—— Essays. 7 vols.
—— Essays. A New and Revised Edition, on tinted paper. 6 vols.
Mackintosh's (Sir James) Essays.
Madge.
Mahan's Answer to Colenso.
—— Numerals of Scripture.
Mahon's England. 2 vols.
Maiu's Novum Testamentum Græce.
Mandeville's New Series of Readers.
1. Primary Reader.
2. Second Reader.
3. Third Reader.
4. Fourth Reader.
5. Fifth Reader.
Mandeville's Course of Reading.
——— Reading and Oratory.
——— First Spanish Reader.
——— Second Spanish Reader.
——— Third Spanish Reader.
Magnall's Historical Questions.
Man's Cry and God's Gracious Answer.
Manners' At Home and Abroad.
——— Sedgemoor.
Manning's Temporal Mission of the Holy Ghost.
——— The Reunion of Christendom.
Manual of Matrimony.
Markham's History of England.
Marrayat's Africa.
——— Masterman Ready.
——— Popular Novels. 12 vols.
——— A New and Revised Edition, printed on tinted paper 12 vols.
Marryat's Settlers in Canada.
Marshall's (E. C.) Book of Oratory.
——— First Book of Oratory.
Marshall's (T. W.) Notes on Episcopacy.
Marsh's Double Entry Book-keeping.
—— Single Entry Book-keeping.
—— Bank Book-keeping.
—— Book-keeping (in Spanish).
—— Blank Books for Double Entry. 6 books in set.
—— Do. for Single Entry. 6 books in set.
Martha's Hooks and Eyes.
Martineau's Crofton Boys.
——— Peasant and Prince.
Mary Lee.
Mary Staunton.
Mathews on Whist.
Mayhew's Illustrated Horse Docto
May's Bertram Noel.
—— Louis' School Days.
—— Mortimer's College Life.
—— Sunshine of Greystone.
McCormick's Visit to Sebastopol.

McIntosh's Aunt Kitty's Tales.
—— Charms and Counter Charms.
—— Evenings at Donaldson Manor.
—— Lofty and Lowly. 2 vols.
—— Maggie and Emma.
—— Meta Gray.
—— Two Lives.
—— Two Pictures.
—— New Juvenile Library. 7 vols. in case.
McLee's Alphabets.
McWhorter's Church Essays.
Meadows' Italian Dictionary.
Memoirs of Catharine II.
Merchant of Venice.
Merivale's History of the Romans. 7 vols.
Conversion of the Roman Empire.
" " Northern Nations.
Merry Christmas Book.
Michelet's France. 2 vols.
Milhouse's Italian Dictionary. 2 vols.
Mill's Political Economy. 2 vols.
Milledulcia.
Milton's Poems.
—— Paradise Lost.
Miniature Library. 27 vols.
Ministry of Life.
Minturn's Travels in India.
Modern British Essayists. 8 vols.
Modet's Light.
Moore's Revolutionary Ballads.
Moore's (George H.) Notes on the History of Slavery in Massachusetts.
Moore's (Thos.) Irish Melodies.
Moore's (Thos.) Memoirs and Journal. 2 vols.
—— Lallah Rookh.
—— Poems. 1 vol., cheap edition.
—— Do., on fine tinted paper.
Morales' Spanish Reader.
Moran on Money.
More's Practical Piety. 2 vols.
—— Private Devotions.
—— Domestic Tales.
—— Rural Tales.
—— Village Tales. 2 vols. in 1.
Morin's Practical Mechanics.
Morphy's Chess Games.
—— Triumphs.
Mulligan's English Grammar.
My Cave Life in Vicksburg.

Napoleon Bonaparte, by F. de l'Ardeche.
Napoleon Correspondence. 2 vols.
New Fairy Stories.
Newcomb on Financial Policy.
Newman's Apologia Pro Vita Sua.
—— Sermons.
New Testament, with engravings on wood from designs by the ancient masters. 1 vol.
New Testament, with Comment by E. Churton and W. B. Jones. 2 vols.
New York City Banks.
New York Picture Galleries.
Nightcap Series of Juveniles. 6 vols. in case.
Nightingale on Nursing.
Novum Testamentum, interprete Beza.
Nueva Biblioteca de la Risa.
Nuovo Tesoro di Schergos.
Nursery Basket.

O'Callaghan's New Netherlands. 2 vols.
Œhlschlager's German Reader.
Ogilby on Lay Baptism.
Oldfellow's Uncle Nat.
Oliphant's Katmandu.
Ollendorff's English Grammar for Spaniards.
A Key to the Exercises.
—— English Grammar for Germans.
A Key to the Exercises.
—— French Grammar, by Jewett.
A Key to the Exercises.
—— French Grammar, by Value.
A Key to the Exercises.
—— French Grammar for Spaniards.
Key to the same.
—— German Grammar.
A Key to the Exercises.
—— Italian Grammar.
A Key to the Exercises.
—— Spanish Grammar.
A Key to the Exercises.
Ortografia.
Ordronaux' Hints on Health.
Oriental Library. 5 vols. in case.
Osgood's Hearthstone.
—— Mile Stones.
Ostervald's Nouveau Testament.
Otis' Landscapes. 1 vol.
—— The same, in 6 parts.
—— Studies of Animals. 1 vol.
—— Studies of Animals. 6 parts.
Overman's Metallurgy.
Owen's (Jno. J.) Acts of the Apostles.
—— Greek Reader.
—— Homer's Odyssey.
—— Homer's Iliad.
—— Thucydides.
—— Xenophon's Anabasis.
—— Xenophon's Cyropædia.
Owen's Penmanship. 8 books.

Paez' Geografia del Mundo.
Pages and Pictures. From the writings of James Fenimore Cooper.
Paine's Tent and Harem.
Palenzuela's Gramatica Inglesa.
Key to the same.
Palmer's Book-keeping.

Parker's Critical and Miscellaneous Writings.
—— Speeches and Addresses. 3 vols.
—— Additional Speeches. 2 vols.
—— Sermons of Theism.
—— Ten Sermons.
—— Trial and Defence.
—— Two Christmas Celebrations.
—— Works. 2 vols.
—— (Life of Theodore). 2 vols.
Parley's Faggots for the Fireside.
—— Present for all Seasons.
Parley's Wanderers by Sea and Land.
Patton's History of the United States.
Paul and Virginia.
Pearson on the Creed.
Perkins' Primary Arithmetic.
—— Elementary Arithmetic.
—— Practical Arithmetic.
—— The same, in Spanish.
—— A Key to Practical Arithmetic.
—— Higher Arithmetic.
—— Algebra.
—— Higher Algebra.
—— Geometry.
—— Higher Geometry.
—— Plane Trigonometry.
Perry's Americans in Japan.
—— Expedition to the China Seas and Japan.
Petit's Household Mysteries.
Peyrac's Comment on Parle à Paris.
Phelan on Billiards.
Phœnixiana.
Picture Gallery, in Spanish.
Pickell's Narrative. History of the Potomac Company.
Planches' Lead Diseases.
Plato's Apology.
Poetical Gems. Blue and Gold. 6 vols. in case.
Poets' Gallery.
Pollok's Poems.
Pomeroy's Municipal Law.
Pope's Poems.
Porter's Scottish Chiefs.
Portraits of my Married Friends.
Practical Cook Book.
Pratt's Dawnings of Genius.
Prince Charlie.
Pulpit Cyclopædia and Minister's Companion.
Punch's Pocket-Book of Fun.
Punchinello.
Pure Gold.
Pusey's Eirenicon.
Putz's Ancient Geography.
—— Mediæval Geography.
—— Modern Geography.

Quackenbos' First Book in English Grammar.
—— English Grammar.
—— First Lessons on Composition.
Quackenbos' Advanced Course of Composition and Rhetoric.
—— Natural Philosophy.
—— Primary History.
—— History of the United States.
—— Primary Arithmetic.
—— Elementary Arithmetic.
—— Practical Arithmetic.
Queens of England: a Series of Portraits.

Railway Anecdote Book.
Rawlinson's Herodotus. 4 vols.
Recreative Readings in French.
Reid's English Dictionary.
Reminiscences of a Zouave.
Replies to Essays and Reviews.
Republican Court.
Report on the Hygienic Condition of New York City.
Report of the United States Revenue Commission.
Reynard the Fox. After the version of Goethe.
Reynolds on Hand-Railings.
Rice's (Harvey) Poems.
Richards' At Home and Abroad.
—— Pleasure and Profit.
—— Harry's Vacation.
—— Electron.
Ricord's Youth's Grammar.
Ripalda's Spanish Catechism.
Robbins' Book of Poetry.
—— Guide to Knowledge.
Robertson's English Course for Spaniards, with Key.
Roemer's First French Reader.
—— Second French Reader.
—— Polyglot Readers—comprising English Text; French, German, Spanish, and Italian Translations.
Rosa Mystica.
Rosales' Caton Christiana.
Round the Block.
Rowan's French Reader.
—— French Revolution. 2 vols.
Royo's Instruccion Moral.

St. Pierre's Paul and Virginia.
Saintaine's Picciola. (In French.)
Sallust, with Notes.
Sampson's Brief Remarker.
Sandham's Twin Sisters.
Sanitary Condition of New York.
Sarmiento's Lectura Gradual.
Savarin's Hand-Book of Dining.
Schedel's Emancipation of Faith. 2 vols.
Schmidt's Ancient Geography.
Schmucker's History of the Four Georges.
Schwegler's History of Philosophy.
Scott's Lady of the Lake.
—— Lay of the Last Minstrel.

www.ingramcontent.com/pod-product-compliance
Lightning Source LLC
LaVergne TN
LVHW021407110826
845150LV00007B/1817

* 9 7 8 1 4 2 5 5 1 2 0 7 1 *